LAUREL and HARDY
CLOWN PRINCES OF COMEDY

BRUCE CROWTHER

Foreword by
ERNIE WISE

COLUMBUS BOOKS
LONDON

First published in Great Britain in 1987 by
Columbus Books Limited
19-23 Ludgate Hill, London EC4M 7PD

Designed by Kirby-Sessions, London

British Library Cataloguing in Publication Data
Crowther, Bruce
    Laurel and Hardy: clown princes of
    comedy.
    1. Hardy, Oliver   2. Laurel, Stan
    3. Moving-picture actors and actresses——
    United States——Biography
    I. Title
    791.43′028′0922   PN2287.L285

    ISBN 0–86287–344–4

Phototypeset by Falcon Graphic Art Ltd
Wallington, Surrey
Printed and bound by
R.J. Acford, Chichester, Sussex

LAUREL and HARDY
CLOWN PRINCES OF COMEDY

'93

791
.43
028
0922
Cro

Crowther, Bruce, 1933–
   Laurel and Hardy : clown princes of comedy /
Bruce Crowther ; foreword by Ernie Wise. -- London :
Columbus, 1987.
   192 p. : ill.

Filmography: p. 177–185.
Discography: p. 187.
Bibliography: p. 188.
02962934 ISBN:0862873444 (pbk.) :

1. Hardy, Oliver, 1892–1957. 2. Laurel, Stan. 3.
Motion picture actors and actresses – United States –
Biography. I. Title

130

88 MAY 26

Contents

FOREWORD 7

1 **Way Out West:** Hal Roach Productions 9

2 **Them Thar Hills:** Origins and Early Hollywood 11

3 **Helpmates:** Development of a Partnership 29

4 **Their Purple Moment:** the Silent Classics 37

5 **Unaccustomed As We Are:** the Classic Talkies 63

6 **Their First Mistake:** End of an Era 101

7 **Our Relations:** Chaplin, Keaton and Lloyd 121

8 **Me and My Pal:** Style, Technique and Influence 132

9 **Nothing But Trouble:** the Big Studio Years 137

10 **On the Loose:** the Laurel and Hardy
Stock Company 157

11 **The Finishing Touch:** Final Curtains 165

12 **Leave 'Em Laughing:** Happy Memories 171

FILMOGRAPHY 177

LAUREL AND HARDY IN BRITAIN 186

SELECT DISCOGRAPHY 187

BIBLIOGRAPHY 188

ACKNOWLEDGEMENTS 189

PICTURE CREDITS 189

INDEX 190

Foreword

It's as if I grew up with Laurel and Hardy. I saw most of their films at the local cinema when I was a kid. They made me laugh then and they still do. I wasn't alone then. They came together on the screen in 1927 and made millions laugh, even in the bad times of the Depression. And I'm certainly not alone in laughing at them now.

Odd, really, because they're a pair of losers but, let's face it, that makes it easier for people to identify with them. What's more they always end up the way they began, as pals, prepared to face the world together. Hardy, big and bossy, bullying poor old Laurel.

I did manage to see them perform live, at the Embassy theatre, Peterborough. They were close to the end of their career and their sketch was not very good – but it was enough just to see them, two master craftsmen at work.

Sadly, I never met them, but in 1985, in Los Angeles, I met Stan's daughter, Lois. It was at a gathering of Laurel and Hardy fans on the anniversary of Stan's birthday. There was a film show, and one of the items was a tribute film to Stan and Ollie, produced by Robert Vass for the BBC and for which Eric and I had done the commentary.

It goes without saying that Eric and I were greatly influenced by Laurel and Hardy: looks at the camera; my affected superiority over Eric; his pretended dumbness; the way I crawled to the big stars on our TV show; the belief I had in the great plays wot I wrote and how Eric went along with it knowing all the time that they were rubbish. We even shared a double bed, just like Stan and Ollie. (In later years, we changed: I became softer and Eric more pushy. I think this was the change of writers from Hills and Green to Eddie Braben.)

Great double-acts are extremely rare. It's a million-to-one chance that two people can get together and this miracle happens. It happened with Laurel and Hardy. They have stood the test of time (even today's kids love them, for all their computer games and sophistication).

They were just two boys, trying to make people laugh – how they succeeded! But above and beyond all the laughter, one quality which came over loud and clear was that they loved each other – on and off the screen – and because of that we loved them. Many of us still do.

Ernie Wise

CHAPTER ONE

Way Out West

Hal Roach Productions

'We'd try one thing, it wasn't funny; we'd try
something else.'

Hal Roach

It was not simply good luck when, in 1927, Stan Laurel and Oliver Hardy were co-starred in *Putting Pants on Philip*. Neither was it the first time they had worked together in a movie. Their 'partnership' is not as well emphasized here as it was in *Duck Soup* and *Do Detectives Think?*, which were made earlier in the year. Indeed, *Philip* has no in-series distinction but it was a deliberate attempt to formalize the teaming of two remarkable individual comic talents which might possibly be enhanced if they worked together. But not even the most perceptive of this film's makers at Hal Roach Studios can have foreseen that those separate talents, demonstrably excellent though they were, would add up to the finest comedy duo in the history of the movies.

When Stan Laurel and Oliver Hardy came together on the Roach lot, each had a great deal to offer the other although at first neither seemed to be aware of this. Indeed, there is some evidence that Stan was understandably uneasy at being teamed with anyone: not for any personal reason but, having been either the leading component of a vaudeville troupe or a leading actor in films, Stan saw no good reason to share the limelight.

Credit for the initiative to team 'the Boys', as they came to be known on the lot, has been claimed by or for Hal Roach, the head of the studio, and for Leo McCarey, one of his assistants and, at the time, comedy supervisor. Certainly, what happened when the teaming was a fact, and who played the greatest role in its success, has become the centre of considerable dispute in recent years.

In his pioneering and warmly intimate books

on the Boys, *Mr Laurel and Mr Hardy* and *The Comedy World of Stan Laurel*, John McCabe comes down with considerable firmness on the side of Stan Laurel as being the major force behind the Boys' success. The fact that Professor McCabe's books owed their origins to lengthy conversations between the author and Stan led some to doubt their impartiality. What emerges, however, from reported conversations, casual asides and detailed study of their films is that more significant than the initial decision to team Laurel with Hardy is the subsequent development of their on-screen characters.

Character development by comics on the lot was an important part of the success of the films made by Hal Roach Productions. This facet of the Roach policy is in marked contrast with that of the other great master of comedy film production, Mack Sennett. Roach's comics had to be readily identifiable, and to achieve this individual psychological traits were established: Ollie became the pompous, officious busybody while Stan took on the role of mewling incompetent. The fact that for all his self-assurance Ollie is just as dumb as Stan gave the characters and their audience a great deal upon which to feed.

However, Hal Roach's concern with characterization should not be considered as any more than one aspect of his overall policy, for his control of the detail of the enormous number of things happening at his studio at the time appears, understandably, to have been delegated. He has remarked that 'great comedians imitate children' and includes Chaplin and Langdon in his comment. While it is easy to support the statement with regard to Langdon it is much less tenable with Chaplin. Pursuing the theme with specific regard to Laurel and Hardy he appears to be on stronger ground but is still uncertain: 'Hardy's action with the tie, Laurel's scratching his head, these are the actions of a child.' In fact, Stan's head-scratching is not so much a child's gesture as that of the classic buffoon. Significantly, Stan hated the famous cry, which *is* a child's action. He knew that this was not always in keeping with the character.

Aside from Roach and the Boys themselves, among those who were around to witness events at Hal Roach Productions during the early weeks of Laurel and Hardy's development (and it is important to remember that it happened fast), it is Leo McCarey who has usually received most attention.

McCarey's role as supervisor suggests that he must have exercised considerable influence upon the content and form of the Boys' films in their formative years. His association with them ended in 1930, after which his career went in other directions. Laurel and Hardy continued to build upon that pre-1930 groundwork throughout most of their association with Hal Roach Productions, which ended in 1940. Only three men were present during this entire period: Hal Roach, Oliver Hardy and Stan Laurel.

Oliver Hardy openly avoided serious involvement in the production side of their work and ingenuously deferred to Stan when asked about their contributory roles. 'If Stan says it's funny, I do it,' he remarked to the British entertainer Ray Alan, who worked with the Boys in the 1950s. As a result of his attitude, Hardy is frequently dismissed in discussions regarding the making of the team. He portrayed the amiably pompous buffoon so well on-screen that it is easy to regard him as such off-screen too. Yet his grasp of both the fundamentals and the detail of film-making is so evident in all his screen appearances from the early 1920s onwards that, regardless of his self-deprecation, he must be taken as a man who knew exactly what he was doing. His contributions to the team were invaluable, although perhaps more practical than creative.

If Hardy also chose to let Stan beaver away at the studios after the day's shooting was over it would be wrong to take this as a sign of either lack of interest or incompetence. Unlike Stan, who lived to work, Oliver Hardy clearly worked in order that he might live his life in other ways. This being so, his behaviour makes plain good sense. No doubt he calculated that the extra money Stan earned for his extra work was but small recompense for the valuable time that could be spent playing golf, going racing or, later, when his private life was settled, staying home with his wife.

However skilled Roach was in producing films, and he was certainly that, it is difficult to see how he could have spared time from the demands of running one of Hollywood's busiest studios in order to concern himself with day-to-day matters such as gag construction and the individual touches that Laurel and Hardy so quickly developed.

Of the three continuing presences during the highly productive 13-year period at the studio only Stan Laurel can be truly described as a constantly creative one. He brought to the partnership not only his enormous talents as a performer but also his often overlooked qualities as a writer, director, editor and contributor of an endless succession of ideas for gags. That he often culled these from memories of his years on the stage does not in any way diminish his input. In the final Roach years, when the overall quality of the Boys' work was in decline and Hal Roach himself obviously had his mind on other things, the gags were continually undergoing refinement and polishing. That the movies in which these gems gleamed were sometimes poor should not detract from Laurel's contribution.

What appears on-screen, then – an imperfect partnership of snapping incompetents, forever at odds with a chaotic and cockeyed world – is in direct contrast to the reality, a perfect combination of two complementary talents: Stan Laurel, a creative comic mind with few peers, who often touched genius; and Oliver Hardy, a highly skilled actor with a superbly developed gift for comedy.

Separately only some measure of their talents was realized. Together they became, quite simply, the funniest duo in the history of comedy.

CHAPTER TWO

Them Thar Hills

Origins and Early Hollywood

'In the vaudeville house the film clowns learned
valuable physical lessons that they never
forgot . . .'

Gerald Mast

Stan Laurel was born in Ulverston, Lancashire, England on 16 June 1890. Ulverston is a small, unexceptional town some thirty miles north of Blackpool and bordering upon, but not improved by, the Lake District. Stan's parents, Arthur and Margaret Jefferson (Jeff and Madge), were struggling actors. The house in which their son Arthur Stanley was born was not their own. It was the home of Madge's parents and was small enough to be overcrowded by the two families. The Jeffersons had an older boy and after Stan came a girl, but by then Jeff and Madge had moved to North Shields, where Jeff had been appointed manager of the Theatre Royal.

The Jeffersons' professional life really took off with Jeff newly-launched on his career as theatrical impresario and, soon, owner of a chain of theatres in the north of England. Domestically things were less happy as the birth of another son damaged Madge's health permanently. For young Stan those early years were a mixture of the comparatively secure and certainly warm family life with his grandparents in Ulverston and the emotional desert of life at his boarding school at Bishop Auckland. The school was, however, only some 30 miles from North Shields, and therefore close enough for him to visit his father's theatre.

Stan's interest in the scholastic life was decidedly minimal. He proved the point with an engagingly less-than-grammatical comment about his schooldays in a letter written many years later to friends, Mr and Mrs Short, in the North-East. 'I think I have the honour,' he wrote, 'of been the worst scholar that ever attended there.'

Stan's life was interspersed with sporadic visits to his parents, which involved travelling to many major cities in the north of England, for by now Jeff's reputation was spreading. He was now respectfully known as A. J. by the staff of the half dozen or more theatres which he leased. He also became managing director of the North British Animated Picture Company.

Domestically, affairs were less settled. Stan's biographer, Fred Guiles, suggests that Stan was uneasy at his father's roving eye and that his casual sexual relationships with actresses were disturbing to a young boy deeply devoted to his mother.

However, Stan's enthusiasm for the theatre soon developed into an obsession. He spent every moment he could backstage, where his father encouraged him, expecting Stan to follow him in management. Over the years, although his reputation continued to gain ground, A. J. lost a great deal of money. In another of Stan's letters, now in public care and published in Jenny Owen-Pawson's book *Laurel Before Hardy*, he recalls that his father invested a great deal of money in the New Theatre Royal in Blythe. Ahead of its time, it had 'electric lighting, the floors were carpeted, tip up red velvet chairs etc. Lifts instead of stairs to the Balcony & Gallery [and it] even had a nursery with nurses in attendance to take care of the children . . .' But all this, together with the evening dress and smart uniforms worn by the orchestra, stage crew and programme-sellers, frightened off many of the customary working-class audience. They thought that they too had to dress up, 'so the only time they did come was Saturday night, wearing their Sunday suit!' The financial damage was shattering and A. J. had to give up the theatres he leased to take a job as manager of Glasgow's Metropole Theatre.

In 1901 Stan was taken there too, and for the first time lived more or less consistently with his family. Already he was displaying an eagerness for the theatrical life. Earlier he had formed, for family pleasure only, the Stanley Jefferson Amateur Dramatic Society. In Glasgow, his ambition drove him on to stronger stuff.

The Metropole, located in Stockwell Street, Glasgow South, was one of Scotland's most important theatres. It had first opened its doors on 29 December 1862, when it was known as the Scotia Music Hall (in the tradition of the day it backed on to a popular public house, in this case the Scotia). In the 1890s the Scotia was managed by H. E. Moss – of the later Moss Empires – and was closed briefly when the Moss Empire was opened in 1897. It reopened the following year as the Metropole and after his arrival three years later A. J. was soon as famous in Scotland as he had been south of the border.

By the time Stan was 16 he had abandoned his education and was working backstage for his father, but his burning ambition was to play on-stage. He had written a sketch which he eventually plucked up the courage to perform, not at his father's theatre but at a Glasgow music hall known as Pickard's. He had not told his father his plans but by a stroke of purest coincidence A. J. chose the night of Stan's début to stroll along from the Metropole to Pickard's and thus saw and heard the act – and the applause.

In later years Stan recalled for John McCabe that his act was 'just bloody awful', but it was the applause that counted even if, as Stan continued, 'this was because the audience felt sorry' for the slightly-built young beginner.

The fortuitous presence of A. J. helped greatly because, having seen his son perform he could and did write a letter of introduction to other managers and impresarios. The word of Arthur Jefferson carried considerable weight, even in London.

Stan's first professional job was with Levy and Cardwell's Pantomimes. As stage manager, he toured England in 1907 with *Sleeping Beauty*, in the cast of which was Wee Georgie Wood, a diminutive comedian whose stature allowed him to work the music halls and variety theatres of England as a 'child' for more than half a century.

Stan followed this with brief appearances as a single and tours in straight drama but was then offered the opportunity to join Fred Karno's talented army of music-hall performers.

An offer from Karno, while notable for the stinginess of the pay, was an unimaginable dream for a young, would-be comic. In the English music halls of the day, Karno was the undisputed top of the bill. His troupe was also the training ground for the best pantomimists, acrobats and comic entertainers.

A young Londoner named Charlie Chaplin was already a highly popular member of the Karno troupe and soon Stan Jefferson was understudying him. Stan's opportunity to play a leading role came when Chaplin turned down the lead in the show *Jimmy the Fearless*, but Stan's success in this was short-lived when Chaplin took over. Aware of Chaplin's almost paranoid reluctance to let anyone take credit for anything when he was around, most latterday observers have suggested that he demanded the role after seeing just how much a threat Stan presented. Another version suggests Chaplin took the role only when it fell vacant, while Fred Karno's biographer, J. P. Gallagher, suggests that Chaplin merely admitted he had been wrong and wished he had accepted the role. This suited Karno, who had other plans for Stan, and he promptly gave the part to Charlie. Whatever the truth of this incident, undoubtedly Fred Karno had in his troupe at one time two of the tiny handful of true comic geniuses of the century.

The show in which Stan regularly understudied Chaplin was *Mumming Birds*, a burlesque of a 'typical' music-hall bill with members of the cast acting as noisily aggressive (and in Chaplin's case, drunken) members of the audience. As the acts came on, each worse than the one before, the 'audience' would roar its disapproval. For the troupe it was an opportunity to perform all the worst routines that filled the bottom half of music-hall bills, deride them openly and get in a few digs at the frequently churlish behaviour of real music-hall audiences in the less salubrious venues.

Ray Alan's father, Albert Whyberd, was assistant stage manager at the Queen's Theatre, Poplar, East London, and recalled Stan taking over from Chaplin. 'He was much more believable, much funnier, not so theatrical. Stan put in a few bits of business that Karno quite liked but Chaplin couldn't do them as effectively. There was a tumble over the edge of the box and back again that Chaplin couldn't do in those days.' Doubtless such occurrences helped fuel the sense of rivalry which Chaplin began to nurture.

Mumming Birds was enormously successful, so much so that Karno was invited to take the show to America. In 1910 two companies crossed the Atlantic. Stan's mother had died in Glasgow in 1908, leaving him depressed and unhappy for months. Later remarks suggest he considered his father to be responsible for her decline into ill-health. Although he never became estranged from A. J., his family ties took second place to the ambitions he was slowly but surely fulfilling. When the trip to America was announced he didn't hesitate.

For two members of the second Karno company, Charlie Chaplin and Stan Jefferson, the journey was the first step to international fame.

The two men, leading comic actor and understudy, shared cheap lodgings in New York and elsewhere as the company toured (although Cha-

plin's marked disinclination to allow credit to pass to anyone else caused him to omit mention of Stan and many others from his autobiography). The show was called *The Wow-Wows* but was much less successful than *Mumming Birds* and when the company left New York it switched over to the more dependable show, changing its title to *A Night in an English Music-hall.*

Among the places played by the troupe was Los Angeles, where already film-makers were taking advantage of the sunshine. So far, however, there was no real film colony in Hollywood.

The pay Stan and the others received was so poor that he eventually demanded a raise, but when Alf Reeves, the troupe's manager, wired Karno in London for permission to increase Stan's salary it was refused. Consequently Stan quit the troupe in Colorado Springs and with the aid of a loan from A. J. headed back home to England.

With a new sketch he had devised Stan formed an act with Arthur Dandoe, also out of favour with Karno. When Dandoe moved on, Stan

Stan Laurel (extreme left, second row) and Charlie Chaplin (in lifebelt) on their way to conquer America in 1910. Fred Karno Jr is between Stan and Charlie, Arthur Dandoe on Chaplin's left.

Oliver Hardy paying the price of mischief in an early film role.

Oliver Hardy answering back in another early film.

teamed up with new partners, Ted Leo and Bob Read, and worked English and Continental halls – with disastrous results, however. Broke and weak with hunger, Stan beat a forlorn retreat, borrowed money from his older brother, Gordon, who was now following in A. J.'s footsteps in theatrical management, and temporarily abandoned his ambitions. He prepared instead to live out his theatrical life as a player of bit parts.

Then he learned that Karno was sending *A Night in an English Music-hall* back to America and wanted him as Chaplin's understudy. What is more, he would pay the previously demanded higher salary. In 1912, his ambition and enthusiasm re-ignited, Stan set sail once more. He would not return to England for two decades, by which time he had long been a star.

It did not happen quite as simply as that; indeed, it was anything but a simple transition, even though Chaplin appears never to have had many doubts that *he* would succeed. Stan Laurel recalled for John McCabe that on their first visit,

in 1910, as their ship, the SS *Cairnrona*, came in sight of land, Chaplin shouted: 'America, I am coming to conquer you!' For Stan, this second arrival in America was the first step on a road which proved to be long, hard and, like any later Hollywood showbiz saga, paved with pitfalls as well as good intentions.

When Chaplin was attracted to California by offers from Mack Sennett the Karno tour quickly folded. American audiences wanted to see Chaplin and neither they nor the bookers were impressed by claims that there were others who could play his part effectively.

When the troupe returned to England Stan elected to stay behind and try his hand in vaudeville. Initially, he worked with Karno colleagues Edgar and Wren Hurley in an act named the Keystone Trio (after an increasingly famous silent movie company), in which he openly imitated Chaplin, the new star of Keystone. When the trio split up Stan replaced his earlier partners with a couple he had met on tour, Alice and

Stan Laurel in Lucky Dog.

Baldwin Cooke. The act, now renamed the Stan Jefferson Trio, continued playing vaudeville theatres throughout North America.

Although Stan and his new partners developed a strong and ultimately lasting bond of friendship, Stan's sometimes erratic behaviour caused passing problems. In 1917 the act was folded by Stan, apparently at the behest of a lady with whom he had formed a strong attachment. The young vaudevillean already had a well-developed eye for the ladies, an attribute which would lead him into serious domestic and emotional crises in the years to come. The lady concerned, Mae Dahlberg, broke up the act but she also helped him constructively by devising a new stage name to replace the thirteen-lettered Stan Jefferson: Stan Laurel.

Later in 1917, Stan and Mae were appearing in Los Angeles when he was invited to make a film. This was *Nuts in May*, in which Stan showed sufficient promise for Universal to sign him for a short string of one-reelers featuring him in the role of Hickory Hiram. The films were not especially successful, but he made more short comedies for Universal in which Mae Dahlberg also appeared, to the general detriment of the films and Stan. Although most film comedy of the time was broad, Mae was crude, which offended many in the audience, and had limited talent as a performer, which held Stan back. Nevertheless, despite their shortcomings, the films attracted attention from both the public and other film-makers, among them Gilbert M. Anderson (Broncho Billy of early western movie fame and later the 'ay' in the Essanay film company), who hired Stan for a comedy short, *Lucky Dog* (1917), in which a small role went to a large, amiable actor named Oliver Hardy.

Hardy was born in the Deep South, in Harlem, Georgia on 18 January 1892. His given name was Norvell, but after his father's death he added his first name. Oliver Hardy Sr was a lawyer and had been a leading figure in local politics. Although his death reduced the family's circumstances it was far from being poor. While Oliver was still a young boy the family moved to a small hotel, the Baldwin in Madison, Georgia, which Mrs Hardy bought soon after she was widowed.

A big child, Oliver was always amiable and friendly, although reputedly he did have a rarely displayed temper, mostly reserved for his activities as umpire at his home town's baseball games.

Blessed with an attractive singing voice, he was

Unshaven Oliver Hardy samples a banana while Larry Semon fishes for bigger fruit. Some sources believe this to be from The Rent Collector, *a film in which Stan Laurel appears. No print of this film was available for viewing but it may be that this is yet another joint appearance by the Boys.*

permitted to join a minstrel troupe when he was only eight years old. Later, in between his law studies at Georgia State University, studying singing at Atlanta Conservatory of Music and military college (from which he ran away), he played in stock companies and worked in small-time vaudeville and also on the showboats which plied American rivers in those days. The long tradition of male quartets attracted him and he sang in a group called the Twentieth Century Four.

When he was 18 the Hardys left Madison and in their new home town of Milledgeville Oliver showed his first interest in the still new-fangled moving pictures by opening a movie theatre. This new world of movies held a powerful fascination for him. In 1913 he travelled to Florida, where the Lubin company had its home and was busily

Oliver Hardy, complete with flyaway moustache and eyebrows, fends off Larry Semon in The Fall Guy.

churning out comedy one-reelers. With Lubin the young but burly Oliver Norvell Hardy found work as a 'heavy'. He also picked up the nickname of 'Babe', which admirably suited his friendly disposition. The nickname stuck firmly for the rest of his life and was used by all his friends and relatives. Although he was for a while billed as 'Babe' and appeared in such films as *Babe's School Days*, the name was soon discontinued in his professional career.

It was in 1913 that Babe married for the first time. His bride was Madelyn Saloshin, but although the marriage did not formally end for several years it had effectively dissolved within a matter of months.

Babe continued working for Lubin (soon to be taken over by Vim) in Florida, with occasional side trips to New York when film work demanded. While in New York he also worked for such rising organizations as Vitagraph, Pathé and Gaumont. In this rather small universe he had become a minor comic star but was restlessly aware that there must be a better future elsewhere in the film world.

Among the numerous two-reelers Babe made was one for Gilbert M. Anderson, *Lucky Dog*. Babe's role was that of a hold-up man who sticks a gun in the ribs of the movie's star, the young English comic Stan Laurel.

The title card which heralded their first meeting on film read, 'Put 'em up, insect, before I comb your hair with lead.' That Stan should despatch the hold-up man with a swift kick on the seat of his pants was no magical foresight of their later partnership but simply a standard piece of silent comedy business.

For Babe it was soon apparent that if he was to continue his movie career – and he never seems to have had any doubt whatsoever that this was how he would spend his life – then Hollywood was the place to be. So he headed westwards, where his substantial presence was soon in as much demand as ever before. Moviemakers then (as now) regularly used readily identifiable stereotypes. The bad guy in a film was known as the 'heavy' primarily because he took a role which required him to exert powerful dramatic pressure. By casting in such roles actors who were literally of heavy build a swift communication of intent was made to the audience. In comedies this was especially useful as, with rare exceptions, the comic lead was usually small.

In one place or another Babe made an uncountable number of films between 1914 and his eventual teaming with Stan Laurel. Credit for bit-part players was not commonplace and as many films have been lost over the years complete accuracy is impossible, but Richard W. Bann, the Boys' most assiduous filmographer, has accounted for more than 200.

Among Hardy's roles were the heavy in the Jimmy Aubrey Comedies (Aubrey was yet another English graduate of the Fred Karno school); he played the heavy to Billy West, the most successful Chaplin impersonator of the day (some of the West comedies were directed by Charles Parrott, better known as comedian Charley Chase). The West comedies were made for King Bee and at one point Babe Hardy was reported to have been offered more money the heavier he became. In one King Bee production, *Playmates* (1918), he and Billy West tackle the roles of children, a foretaste of a much later Laurel and Hardy venture. Among Babe's most successful early films were those in which he played foil to Larry Semon at Vitagraph. In *The Sawmill* (1922), one of Semon's best movies, he played the irate foreman whose job (to say nothing of his life) is at risk thanks to Semon's incompetent progress around the factory in which the tale is set. In another Semon comedy, *Kid Speed* (1924), Babe shared the screen with James J. Corbett, the noted prizefighter, and in another, *The Wizard of Oz* (1925), he took the role of the Tin Woodsman. He also made several appearances with cowboy star Buck Jones, including *Gentle Cyclone* (1926).

After his chance appearance in *Lucky Dog* with Hardy, Stan had largely failed to capitalize upon his earlier film work. However, Gilbert M. Anderson had remained convinced that Stan had potential and in 1922 featured him in several comedies which included a memorable skit on that year's hugely successful Rudolph Valentino movie *Blood and Sand*. This was entitled *Mud and Sand*, in which Stan played the role of Rhubarb Vaselino, a matador possessing remarkable *sang-froid*. *Mud and Sand* was so popular that another skit on a 'straight' movie followed during 1923. *When Knights Were Cold* took off Marion Davies's *When Knighthood Was in Flower* (1923) and featured Stan as a highly unlikely swordsman.

Meanwhile, across at the Roach lot, Harold Lloyd had decided to leave and form his own

Stan Laurel in straw boater (4th from left, second row), Hal Roach in shirt sleeves (4th from right, second row) in 1923.

company. Hal Roach had begun in films as an actor in 1912 and when, in 1915, he inherited some money, he formed his own company and promptly took under contract a young actor he had worked with and whom he believed to have great potential. This was Harold Lloyd, but Roach's money ran out before they met with much success. For a while they went their separate ways, Lloyd to Keystone and Roach to Essanay. Then Roach found a backer, contacted Lloyd and began work on the Lonesome Luke series that made Lloyd a star.

Unlike his great rival Mack Sennett, Roach concentrated upon strong storylines and well-structured films. This helped broaden the appeal of his product to the expanding audience of sophisticates.

Roach also differed from Sennett in the extent to which he delegated responsibility. Many direc-

tors, script-writers and gag-men were employed on the Roach lot, often sparked off by ideas from Roach. This helped fuel the later dissension over just how creative Roach really was. Leo McCarey recalled that 'some guy' (clearly a guarded reference to Roach) would come into his room 'and say, "Listen – Laurel and Hardy in a cobbler's shop." I'd say, "Yes? Then what?" and the guy would say, "That's it – take over." '

Roach was also capable of recognizing talent. Before his cameras appeared such gifted artists of the silent screen as Snub Pollard, Will Rogers, Charley Chase and Edgar Kennedy, and he also created the archetypal troupe of child comedy actors, Our Gang. Roach's response to the advent of talking pictures was predictably far-sighted. From that moment on he was no longer Sennett's competitor but out in front on his own.

A few years earlier Roach had used Stan to

Oliver Hardy prepares for battle with Kate Price while Larry Semon sneaks upstairs (The Perfect Clown).

complete a short series of comedies when another star, Toto the clown, had quit. Although Stan had performed well enough Roach had pretty much discounted him from any further work partly because Stan's light blue eyes photographed so palely that he looked blind. Stan was also frequently blind in other ways at this time, it seems. With his career at an uncertain stage, caught as he was between vaudeville and movies, and privately under some strain resulting from his barbed relationship with Mae Dahlberg, Stan had become a heavy drinker. Now, however, with the drinking habit apparently under control, the benefit of new film stock which accommodated the paleness of his eyes, and, no doubt, out of simple desperation, Roach offered Stan more money than Anderson could match.

A trade paper advertisement of 1923 trumpeted: 'A new comedy face, soon to be famous, is

Oliver threatens Larry Semon in The Wizard of Oz . . .

. . . and is threatened by Buck Jones in Gentle Cyclone.

peeking above the horizon . . . His manner, his style and his methods are his own. The name "Stan Laurel" is going to mean a lot more a year from today than it does now.'

Among the films Stan made for Roach during 1923 and 1924 were more skits on famous films of the day. *The Soilers* gently ribbed *The Spoilers* while *Under Two Jags* parodied *Under Two Flags*. *Rupert of Hee Haw* (*Rupert of Hentzau*) and *Monsieur Don't Care* (*Monsieur Beaucaire*) came similarly close in their titles to warn everyone what to expect.

Much more in line with the usual Roach comedy of the period was *Smithy* (1924), in which Stan plays an unemployed incompetent who is hired to work on a building site. Accidentally put in charge of the work, Stan's efforts result in the destruction of the house. Along the way, he wrestles with sticky, flapping roof tiles in a manner reminiscent of Buster Keaton, scampers about energetically – and also displays some interesting characteristics. For one thing, he wears a hat which is similar to the familiar bowler or derby; and there is a moment when he stands, back to camera, hands clasped loosely behind him, quietly surveying the uproar he has unwittingly caused.

This studied calm amidst the chaos was later to become a standard part of his arsenal of techniques. Leo McCarey was already with Roach as gag-writer but was still learning his trade. It seems unlikely that he would have suggested this device to Stan, who was very much in control of this stage of his career. Stan's role on the Roach lot

was more than that of a mere comic actor. He
wrote scripts, devised and developed gags and
directed. But the level of success was not sustained and in the middle of the 1920s Hal Roach
once again let Stan go.

Roach's motives were in part determined by
the success he was enjoying with Our Gang and
Charley Chase. He did not need Stan, especially
as this was a period when America's blue-
stockings were on the lookout for improprieties in
Hollywood. Stan's relationship with Mae Dahlberg was unacceptable by the double standards of
the day. Had they married, things might have
been different. Perhaps fortunately for Stan, who
later showed an alarming enthusiasm for tying the
knot, they could not marry. Mae already had a
husband in Australia.

During this same period Babe Hardy's private
life appeared settled, but this was only a surface

Stan, parodying Rudolph Valentino, in Mud and Sand.

Stan Laurel untidying the office in The Egg.

Marital bliss for Stan in Handy Man.

Stan's swordplay goes awry in When Knights Were Cold.

Another parody: Stan in Under Two Jags *with demure and militant ladies.*

gloss. He had married again, in 1921, but his new wife, Myrtle, took exception to his interest in golf and horse-racing. They kept up the charade for several more years while Babe retained his extra-marital interests, now including a long-lasting relationship with Viola Morse, and Myrtle increasingly sought solace in drink. Nevertheless, onlookers saw what they wanted to see – an apparently happy marriage – and let him alone. Stan, after all, gave them enough to occupy their attentions.

Another film-maker, Joe Rock, was aware of Stan's reputation as a drinker (one that was largely unjustified) and also knew of the complicated ongoing and taxing relationship with Mae Dahlberg. Stan was again fortunate, for Rock was friendly with some of Stan's friends, Perce and Gertrude Pembroke. They worked on Joe Rock and softened his resolve not to hire Stan.

Later in life, when John McCabe and others met him, Stan was a mellow and always amiable individual. In his younger days, when the adrenalin was still surging, he was clearly much less easy-going. Yet the list of his friends is a long one and most remained so for decades, through bad times and good. Unquestionably, despite any human frailties he might have had, he had charm and those qualities which caused people to over-look any less fortunate peccadilloes.

Joe Rock was eventually persuaded to bank on Stan as the star of a series of comedies he planned on making at his newly formed Joe Rock Productions. But before he was wholly content Rock had to be sure Stan would finish the series, which was unlikely with Mae around. As Rock recalled the subsequent events (for the Rosenberg-Silverman book *The Real Tinsel*), his scheming was worthy of latterday TV soap opera. The upshot of it all was that Mae set sail for Australia and her husband with a payoff in cash and jewels, and Stan went to work with considerable enthusiasm, a clearly lighter heart, and, within hours, thanks to Rock's plotting, a new girlfriend.

Although this sounds as if Rock had precipitated a somewhat sordid arrangement, nothing was farther from the truth. Stan and Lois Neilson

Oliver Hardy in Crazy to Act.

hit it off right away and they were soon married. Although there were ups and downs, it was, for nine years, a period of relative stability in Stan's life. He and Lois had a daughter, who was also named Lois, and a son, Stan Jr, who died in infancy.

Audience appreciation of Stan became very apparent during the period he spent with Rock and he was soon tempted back to Hal Roach Productions, where comedies were being spun out of the air with staggering speed and abundance. For the most part Stan was involved in writing and direction and was perfectly happy not to step before the camera. Indeed, he seems to have settled for the role of director as his true métier. Among the films he directed were *Yes, Yes, Nanette!* (1925) and *Enough to Do* (1926), both of which featured Oliver Hardy; the former, a very funny film, also starred James Finlayson, who would loom large in the Boys' later work. In 1924 Hal Roach had hired Hardy to work on various movies, but always in minor roles. Nevertheless, he was no longer automatically cast as the heavy

(although he continued to play villains to good effect). Now he was allowed more comic roles and he began to develop an identifiable screen character with considerably more depth than was the case of many (if not most) of his counterparts. The screen vocabulary Hardy developed included the rueful stare into the camera and the slow, shy smile, both of which would later prove perfectly adaptable and invaluable to his partnership with Stan Laurel.

Fate has a habit of intervening in the world of film-making almost as much as it does in the stories told on the screen. In 1926 an All Stars series comedy, *Get 'Em Young*, was in production with Stan directing and Oliver Hardy playing a butler. One day, Babe called in sick – he had scalded himself in the kitchen – and Stan was prevailed upon to play the role of the butler. He performed this task only with great reluctance and the promise of a raise in salary. Later, Stan would recall for John McCabe that here, for the first time, he deliberately used the whimpering cry he later grew to detest.

When Babe returned to work, Roach put him and Stan into a film version of one of Stan's father's old music-hall sketches. The film was *Duck Soup* (1927), which showed several signs that they might well work out as a team on a more permanent basis.

Other films followed, for which Roach displayed enthusiasm but apparently not too much concern with detail. With the appointment of Leo McCarey as supervisor of the Boys' joint work there was soon a visible coherence and, most importantly, the development of true and consistent characters.

In the case of Stan Laurel, the characterizations of countless music-hall and vaudeville sketches were already in his head. His brain positively teemed with ideas and he had already proved a fast learner of all aspects of the film-maker's art.

In Babe Hardy's case, the character that would soon be loved by millions was by now largely established; no one can seriously claim credit for what was Hardy's own thoughtful development, based in part on a comic-book character, in part on his own ceaseless observation of human activity, in part on his own persona and, most of all, on his complete understanding of the film-making process, learned over many years in the business and his two hundred or more screen roles.

CHAPTER THREE

Helpmates
Development of a Partnership

'It was Hardy's personal rhythm . . . that
determined the new pace at which both men were
to work.'

Walter Kerr

Stan Laurel's early films, like Charlie Chaplin's, bear the imprint of his years on the halls in England. Especially apparent is his perfect command of his body. Everything is there, from a secure grasp of the fundamentals of dancing to the pratfall, as is the seemingly simple yet so difficult art of creating a walk that is not only right for the character but also highly distinctive. There are also such moves as the scissor-kick, which Stan employed to great effect and with great regularity until, and including, *Putting Pants on Philip* (but much less often afterwards when his approach to film-making altered). This and other devices were the physical stock-in-trade of the accomplished music-hall clown.

Additionally, and of crucial importance to the silent clowns of early movies, there is a thorough understanding of the difficult art of mime. This use of the body to express every emotion known to man markedly divides the truly great silent clowns from those who were merely competent.

The English-born silent movie clowns were mightily outnumbered by their American counterparts, most of whom came through the comparable but subtly different school of American vaudeville. Nevertheless, the fact that of the three great kings of those specific arts (Chaplin, Keaton and Lloyd) one had learned his trade in England cannot be ignored. Add in the two crown princes (Laurel and Hardy) and the odds shorten dramatically to two out of five. When it is seen that these two honed their natural talents with Fred Karno, coincidence ceases to be a serious possibility. Quite clearly, the crafts learned in the English music halls, when developed to their fullest

potential, were the very stuff of which silent film comedy was made.

There was even more to Stan Laurel's abilities than those which could be polished on the sometimes punishing stages of English music halls. The working-class audience frequenting some halls made relatively unsophisticated demands upon those who sought to entertain. The periods during which music hall and, later, the variety theatres of England flourished were sufficiently closely matched to eras of deprivation, unemployment and general hardship to suggest very strongly that the halls were used by many of the working class and an escape route, a kind of opiate to which the masses had access. Perhaps this access was no easier than that which they had to religion, but it was certainly much more enjoyable.

For the middle and upper classes who began to move in at about the turn of the century, a different kind of entertainment was needed. Many artists were sufficiently skilled to adapt their acts to suit the change in audience. (An article in *The Sketch* in 1895 demonstrates this as the writer travelled with Marie Lloyd to the five halls she played each night. Her programme for, and the response of, audiences in the East End of London was strikingly different to that in the West End.)

While some audiences demanded, and got, sophistication from the likes of R. G. Knowles, Malcolm Scott, Harry Fragson and Ella Retford, others preferred those acts that cocked a snook at authority, poked fun at a domineering wife and allowed cathartic release in an outburst of violence against either authority or wives or both. In these routines, drunks were seldom derided but became a kind of Everyman released from the sociological bonds that tethered the audience. Little men won out over bullies, henpecked husbands got the better of their wives, cast-down employees beat the boss, drunks fooled the police. No one seriously believed it could happen in the real world, but for a couple of hours on a Saturday night the meek inherited the earth.

If the more sophisticated music-hall entertainer had to wait a while before his style could make its mark in movies, the targets of many music-hall comics were transferred to the screen with barely any change at all. Apart from the source of their fun, the silent film clowns learned the basic structure of their trade. The techniques of music-hall comics, from mime and movement to the ability to take falls without harm (well, almost) proved a major asset for silent movies. Of course, not all the clowns understood the mechanics or the philosophy of what they were doing. For most of them it was enough that they knew *how* to do it. However, a select few did understand, and they became the comic geniuses of the new era of moving pictures.

Studying the early films of Chaplin and Laurel, it is hard to decide upon a pecking order. Certainly Chaplin brought a balletic grace to his movements which surpassed Laurel, but Stan compensated by a less cloying use of pathos, the quality which most marred Charlie's work, and persistently employed techniques which were less apparent to the watching audience.

In the early films of Laurel and Chaplin can be seen much of what their music-hall and vaudeville audiences watched in live performances. At first there were awkwardnesses which had to be overcome. The lack of direct contact with the audience was a major hurdle, one which Chaplin overcame within months of beginning in films. He appropriated the camera, playing to it, and hence to the unseen audience whose members he encouraged to conspire with him against the hardships of his world. To some extent Chaplin succeeded in this attempt to bridge the seemingly unbridgeable gap between celluloid character and the real world, but for the most part he remained an other-worldly character, detached and untouchable. Stan Laurel made much less direct use of the camera and in his early films rarely appeared to bridge that gap. That he succeeded

mightily later suggests that between the early films and those he made with Oliver Hardy he learned, or was taught, a significant truth about movie-making which escaped Chaplin. Just as the camera magnifies the finer qualities it also ensures that any insincerity, however deeply buried it might be, is decidedly noticeable to the audience. Maybe it is not immediately apparent but the impression is there, if only at a subconscious level.

On the surface much of Stan's early work is conducted frantically. He charges from one set-piece to the next without logic, without troubling over cause and effect, and with no obvious awareness that the camera represented a warm-blooded, intelligent audience.

When he made his parodies of Valentino and others a marked change occurred as he began to acknowledge his audience's existence and that it had intelligence. For a parody to be successful it must after all, assume some familiarity on the part of the audience with what is being parodied.

By the time he was at Hal Roach's studio on a fairly steady basis, Stan Laurel's understanding of film comedy had grown to such an extent that he was a valuable and valued member of the production side of the company.

In contrast with Stan Laurel, Oliver Hardy was not, strictly speaking, a true comedian. He was a man who could be funny and who was obviously appreciative of fun but he was, and remained, a highly skilled actor who happened to work in comedy. More importantly, he was a *film* actor. Unlike most of his contemporaries, and despite his few youthful appearances on the boards, Hardy had not learned his trade on the live stage. He was a film-maker from the start and this ability, coupled with a perception of what worked on film and what did not, allowed him to bring an advanced degree of understanding to his screen roles.

Like Chaplin and others, he knew the value of a camera look. His rueful or affronted stare into the lens, which became such a joyful addition to the Laurel and Hardy vocabulary, was in use from an early stage in his career. It can be seen, for example, in a photograph taken during the shooting of *Fortune's Mask* (1922), when, between takes, he stares patiently into the lens of the still camera as the director instructs the film's stars. But there is a difference between what Chaplin achieves and what was achieved by Hardy. Chaplin would seek to get the audience on his side, to

Oliver Hardy in playful mood on a frequently used set.

encourage them to be his accomplices in some upcoming assault on another's person or dignity; Oliver Hardy invites the audience's confidence and understanding of the predicament in which he has found himself. It is he alone who has suffered and no one else is in any danger.

Oliver Hardy's awareness of all the manifold problems of the film actor's duties allowed him to bring to any movie on which he worked a high degree of professionalism. At one level he did what all the best professionals do: he arrived on time, he knew his lines, and he hit his marks. At a deeper, perhaps subconscious, level he understood what would work and what would not.

The British entertainer Ernie Wise, for 30 years half of the hugely successful double-act of Morecambe and Wise, has commented that although he watched both Laurel and Hardy it was Hardy he 'found the more interesting of the twosome. Although Laurel was the driving force and created most of their comedy, Oliver Hardy was the better performer.' Perceptively, Ernie Wise asserts that a significant attribute of the partnership was 'the way Hardy projected Laurel.'

Walter Kerr, writing in *The Silent Clowns*, remarks that it was 'Hardy's personal rhythm, a rhythm that has been recognized as that of a "Southern gentleman", that determined the new pace at which both men were to work and to which silent comedy would be forced to accommodate itself.'

At the time of their first teaming perhaps the most important of the early modifications made to the working patterns of Stan and Ollie is that change in pace, especially as applied to Stan. From the frantic behaviour he displayed in many of his early individual films, and which was still occasionally on view after the teaming, he was quite startlingly slowed to a lethargic amble and still later graduated to being almost completely stationary. As Gerald Mast has observed, an 'admirable control of intensity, rhythm and structure . . . had become a comic science at Roach by 1925' and the first 'new' comic to benefit from this scientific approach was not one man but two, Laurel and Hardy.

Oliver Hardy's 'camera look' was already in use in Fortune's Mask. *He is seen here with stars Earle Warren and Patsy Ruth Miller taking direction from director Ensminger.*

The degree to which this new stateliness permeated their work does, however, considerably exceed that of any of the other film-makers at Roach. Here again, Stan Laurel's awareness of his body and the manner in which he could use it to great comic effect are significant factors. This studied deliberateness extends even into the most complex scenes. Even when the duo progresses blindly towards chaos, or confronts the advance of anarchy, careful attention is paid to the tempo of events.

Walter Kerr has found the ideal analogy for what happened in the Laurel and Hardy films when he refers to the turn-of-the-century change in popular music which transformed the quadrille into ragtime. 'Silent film comedy may be said to have begun as ragtime. Laurel and Hardy turned it back into a stately quadrille.' Of all the silent comedians, moreover, no one danced with such a measured tread as Stan Laurel and none displayed such elephantine grace as Oliver Hardy.

Kerr further suggests, and there is ample supporting evidence in all their joint screen work, that the tempo of this dance was set by Hardy. Perhaps this was because he knew it was right, possibly it was because it was simply the best pace for him. Either way, it worked.

Perhaps a case can be argued for Hal Roach as arch-designer of the framework in which the fabric of the partnership could be mounted and for Leo McCarey as the weaver of the backcloth. Given the intensity of the pace at which the team's development took place in the second half of 1927, others must have contributed: a storyline here, a gag there, now a casual suggestion, next an inspired idea. There must have been many who deserve some credit. But at the end of the day all their efforts would have been in vain had Laurel and Hardy not possessed performing talents that allowed them to understand the ideas, translate them into images on-screen and thus capitalize upon the opportunities offered.

When Ernie Wise was asked for his view of the role of writers and others in the career of Laurel and Hardy he commented that in many respects they 'were like Eric and me. The writers thought up the idea of the scene (I might add that the blank sheet of paper is the hardest part), but then they, like us, worked on it and introduced their own bits of dialogue and visual business.'

But there was more, much more, to Laurel and Hardy than the ability to transmute base material into the gold of their joint performances. They needed personal characteristics that would allow them to merge themselves into a team.

In this respect traits which are self-evident in their attitudes towards one another on-screen were of paramount importance; equally important was how they felt about one another off-screen.

In countless off-screen candid photographs the Boys can be seen to have enjoyed the sort of easy relationship which is often unattainable (or at best unsustainable) by other show-business double-acts.

Watching Laurel and Hardy on-screen is to know that theirs was a partnership of genuine, unforced affection even if (or perhaps because) their private lives seldom impinged on one another's. This affection, which became such an integral part of their screen personalities and which was a major factor in their success with audiences, was not designed by Roach or woven by McCarey, although both, like the various directors who worked on the Boys' movies, might have nudged it gently along. It came from inside the two men themselves.

Evidence that the two members of a double-act get along together, by no means guaranteed in show business, cannot be simulated. Ernie Wise comments: 'Some double-acts hated one another. Many used to fight in the dressing room. But I think audiences can feel that in a performance.' For two men to get along is not a matter of hard work, nor is it a matter of good luck. It is 'just two people liking one another'. Laurel and Hardy, like Morecambe and Wise, clearly *did* like one another.

Once the character traits were established much of the team's behaviour and many of their reactions became predictable (and in establishing a comic character of substance there is nothing unimaginative in being predictable). The audience was thus allowed to 'know' what would happen next. In the case of Laurel and Hardy this advance warning of a gag or comic dénouement became as much a part of their success as the gag itself. Knowing that Ollie's dismissal of Stan to a place behind him while *he* opens the door to admit disaster is not less funny because the audience knows disaster lurks outside: it is funnier.

Additionally, the air of unwitting incompetence which trails cloudily around the heads of Stan and Ollie as they embark upon one obviously doomed escapade after another might have become wearying, but their essential 'likeableness' foiled any such danger.

There was also an air about the Boys that continually struck chords with their audience. Although few people in the real world can have known anyone quite as dim as Stan, they all knew an 'Ollie' who would always insist on doing things his way or irritably take over only to prove even more wildly incompetent.

As for that world in which Laurel and Hardy lived, although patently unreal, there was always just a suspicion that it *might* be real – though somewhat cockeyed by comparison with the one outside the movie theatre.

It is in this area that the Boys differ most strikingly from almost all the other silent clowns. Although Chaplin's Little Fellow became an *alter ego* for millions his grip did not retain the next generation of filmgoers. For these later audiences the Little Fellow had no life outside the movie theatre. Subsequent audiences liked or disliked Chaplin, sometimes according to emotional response, sometimes according to rational analysis, sometimes as a result of following trends (often generated by writers on popular culture). Although there is always something to laugh at in Chaplin's work, it is often easier to admire him instead and to regard his films as an intriguing insight into what made people laugh *then*. Then there is Buster Keaton, whose screen life, brilliantly inventive though it always was, was fraught with more perils than those of Pearl White or Douglas Fairbanks. While thrilling at the moment and rightly revered for his technical genius, the adventurers of Buster could not really happen to the 'you and me' which made up the mass audience.

Stan and Ollie could exist outside; they *did* exist, for they were 'you and me' – writ large, perhaps, but recognizable all the same.

In neither typical garb nor perfect harmony in Putting Pants on Philip.

CHAPTER FOUR

Their Purple Moment

The Silent Classics

'They fit as a fiddle to the bow.'

James Agee

In October 1927 *The Jazz Singer* was premièred. From the moment when Al Jolson sang and uttered a few words of dialogue, the days of the silent film were inevitably numbered. But between the release of *Putting Pants on Philip* in December 1927 and May 1929, when their first all-talking picture was released, there was still time for Laurel and Hardy to make more than a score of silent comedies, many of them classics of the genre.

In *Philip* the later traditions of their performances, among them their dress and their personas, are largely absent, although tantalizing glimpses of the future Mr Laurel and Mr Hardy can be seen in the characters of Philip and his uncle Piedmont Mumblethunder.

Attempts to trace the development of the characters who would soon be known throughout the world is complicated by several factors. One is that other films were made by them during 1927 and released ahead of *Philip*. Further complications arose through two companies, Pathé and MGM, releasing Roach pictures simultaneously and not necessarily in the sequence in which they were made. These films still have the Boys playing roles other than Mr Laurel and Mr Hardy and the props and business that became their trademarks are not consistently displayed. In some of their 1927 films their physical characters are quite sharply defined while in others they are all but absent. Looked at in the light of their later work, the behaviour of Philip and his uncle may appear a little strange to latterday audiences.

The film begins with Piedmont Mumblethunder (Hardy) arriving at the dock to meet his Scottish nephew Philip (Laurel). He joins others in deriding a strange-looking kilted individual who is hopelessly resisting an attempted examination by the ship's doctor. Deeply embarrassed to discover that he is laughing at his nephew and pompously conscious of his standing in the town, Piedmont insists that Philip walk behind him. Philip is too cheerfully gregarious for that and, worse, he has the habit of chasing wildly after a passing pretty girl who takes his fancy.

After various adventures which involve the effect of upward draughts of air from sidewalk gratings on Philip's kilt (embarrassing enough for Piedmont at any time but absolutely unendurable after Philip loses his underwear), Piedmont insists that the kilt be replaced with a more seemly pair of trousers. This apparently simple task proves traumatic for Philip, who is virginally naive and deeply distrustful of the tailor's attempt to measure his inside leg.

When Philip lays his kilt in the mud to allow a pretty girl to step safely across the street (an offer she refuses), Piedmont sees this as a way of ruining the offending garment. He steps on the kilt and promptly sinks to his neck in the mud.

Although there are moments in *Philip* that display some of Stan Laurel's later characteristics (the tearful response to the tailor, for example), he is here much more energetic. His character is also somewhat inconsistent, a charge which could rarely, if ever, be levelled at the later performances. For example, the naivety displayed in the tailor's shop scene sits uneasily with his predatory dashes after the girls who cross his path.

For his part, Oliver Hardy's pomposity and

outraged dignity, already used to good effect in scores of films, are clear forerunners of the characteristics he would very quickly perfect.

Some of the sight gags used in *Philip*, the impossibly deep kerbside puddle among them, became eagerly awaited devices in their later films. At this stage, however, none was wholly original but formed a part of the silent film comic's standard vocabulary.

None of the regulars who were to become very much a part of the world of Laurel and Hardy is on-screen here. However, behind the camera are some of the men who played a large, if occasionally disputed, part in their successes. The film was of course produced by Hal Roach; its making was supervised by Leo McCarey, the director was Clyde Bruckman and the cameraman was George Stevens.

The role of director Clyde A. Bruckman, although rarely stressed, cannot be entirely ignored. He worked extensively and significantly with Buster Keaton, as ideas man and gag writer on several films. He co-wrote screenplays including *The Navigator* and *Sherlock Jr.* (both 1924), and co-directed *The General* (1927), now a classic. Apart from his work with Keaton, Bruckman also directed films featuring other major comic talents, including Harold Lloyd and W. C. Fields. Later in his career he also worked with Abbott and Costello, a comedy duo who challenged Laurel and Hardy's popularity in the 1940s. Bruckman's experience and success with these other artists suggest that his role in those early Laurel and Hardy films on which he worked merits a little more attention that has been paid to it in the past. Bruckman's career came to an abrupt halt in 1935, after which he slipped into drunken obscurity. He returned to the headlines only when, after dining in a restaurant knowing he had no money to pay the bill, he shot and killed himself.

Among other films released in 1927 (but before *Philip*) is *Slipping Wives*, in which there is a moment where Ollie, as the butler, attempts to send visiting painter Stan round to the service entrance. The resulting struggle ends with Ollie on the floor, his face in a pool of spilled paint. The ensuing camera look differs here from the later versions only in its brevity. The value of a

With James Finlayson and a whirl of girls in Sugar Daddies.

sustained look as a laughter-maker was not yet fully appreciated. Perhaps this failure to exploit what would eventually become a standard feature of their work lies in the frantic pace of film-making at the time.

Studios often held previews in order to observe audience reactions at first hand. Certainly Hal Roach Productions did so and Stan Laurel, active-ly involved in editing work on the team's early films, used such screenings to help adjust the timing of the gags. However, the early silent comic moviemakers were frequently too busy rushing out two-reelers (running for about twenty-five minutes) every few weeks (or even days) to have time to form a clear idea of why some films had more market appeal than others. Their policy was to stick to known formulae for success, among which was the Hal Roach All Star series of comedies. Individual stars did not neces-sarily shine in these films, mainly because the All Stars were often that in name only, although Stan Laurel and Oliver Hardy were two future excep-tions. When the decision was made to try out Laurel and Hardy as a team, Roach was not expecting to find a comic duo who would become a major attraction. After all, the major comic attractions of the period were solo performers. If the teaming of Laurel and Hardy worked, it would bolster the series; if it did not, they could always try something else.

For *Love 'Em and Weep* (1927) the characters played by Stan and Ollie are subordinate to that played by James Finlayson (making the first of more than thirty films with the Boys). The emergence of a Laurel and Hardy 'stock company' was furthered by the use of Charlie Hall, who appeared in a variety of works ranging over nearly fifty films, and Mae Busch, who would later become a virtual fixture as Mr Hardy's screen wife. The plot, which revolves round a wife's suspicions of her errant husband, was one to which the team returned for a highly successful re-make a few years later, and indeed this theme provided the basis for much of their best work.

After forays into the army (*With Love and Hisses*, 1927), an ocean liner (*Sailors, Beware!*, 1927) and, of course, more marital perils, Stan and Ollie went to jail. In *The Second Hundred*

Trying to escape from prison in The Second Hundred Years.

Still stir-shaven from a spell as jailbirds. With Charley Chase and James Finlayson (Call of the Cuckoos).

Years (1927) they are serving long sentences (*very* long it would seem, for when a fellow convict gloomily announces that he still has forty years to serve, Stan eagerly hands him a letter to mail when he gets out). When Ollie comes up with a plan to escape through a tunnel, Stan is less than convinced it's a good idea but goes along for the crawl. Unfortunately, the tunnel leads right into the warden's office. Another escape attempt succeeds when they leave the prison through the main gates, disguised as painters, and eventually take over a limousine from its occupants, dress in their clothes and continue the journey – which takes them right back to prison. The men they are impersonating, visiting Frenchmen, are guests of the governor (Finlayson). After a dinner party in which their peculiar table manners cause raised eyebrows (or in the case of Finlayson, a manic case of mugging), the escaped convicts' brief taste of freedom is ended.

Although little of their eventual style is evident here, there are distinct signs of their emerging teamwork. Neither of the pair is noticeably the comic to the other's stooge – an endearing, and unusual, quality of their partnership.

However unaware or excessively cautious the studio might have been a few months earlier, the success of the teaming was now apparent, so much so that after the making of *The Second Hundred Years* the Boys were not even allowed to let their hair grow. This explains why they appeared (in supporting roles) in a two-reeler starring Max Davidson, *Call of the Cuckoos* (1927), with their heads still stir-shaven.

In *Do Detectives Think?* and *Hats Off* (both 1927) Stan and Ollie wear derbies while the rest of their wardrobe, especially Ollie's, begins to take on the air of genteel seediness that later became a hallmark. *Hats Off* has not been seen for many years and seems to be lost, but its storyline is known and stills from it exist. The struggle to haul a washing-machine up a long flight of steps was excellent material (re-used a few years later in *The Music Box*, a film which became a classic).

Re-use of material was common practice among film-makers of the time, and later, and is not necessarily a sign of impaired creative thought. Originality was no criterion for quality: if a gag was good there was no reason not to use it again in a later film. By this time, Stan Laurel had begun to exercise considerable influence upon the form and structure of the Boys' films, and especially the gags. If he could improve upon a routine (and Laurel and Hardy regularly honed and polished old jokes), so much the better.

For *The Battle of the Century* (1927) the re-used gag is another old standby of the silent comedy, though not used as frequently as later film-clip compilations would suggest: the pie in the face.

The film begins as a fight picture – Stan is the unlikely prizefighter, Ollie his manager – but its direction changes when Ollie decides he can make more money out of an insurance swindle providing Stan can somehow be inveigled into an accident. When Stan fails to slip on the banana skin Ollie repeatedly throws in front of him, a pie seller (Charlie Hall) steps on it, retaliates, and the film changes direction once more. This final third of the film (all that was shown for many years until the recent discovery of the lost first reel) escalates with sublime insanity until scores of people are hurling hundreds, if not thousands, of pies. But this is no wild, chaotic orgy: the scene possesses a curious symmetry which makes it all seem right. Individual pies are thrown (and filmed) with great care and attention to detail, and this helps make the sequence the best of the half-dozen great pie exchanges in silent comedy.

Once again Hal Roach produced while Leo McCarey supervised, George Stevens photographed and Clyde Bruckman was the director. Among the bit-part players is Anita Garvin, who walks elegantly into the fight scene, slips on a pie and beats a hasty and somewhat less elegant, but perfectly timed, retreat.

The appearance of *The Jazz Singer* towards the end of 1927 had set off wary rumblings in Hollywood, but while many studios were rushing into the new-fangled talkies, the silent comedy film-makers were less sure that their days were numbered. Their doubts were justified for, after all, the comic routines of the early silents were designed to exist without sound. The makers of these films were sure that the old traditions could continue unalloyed by unnecessary dialogue or sound effects. 'Why change it if it ain't broke?' was their motto.

That was not how it was to be, of course, but for a while longer the comedy film-makers were able to continue with their mute ways.

In 1928 the Boys, not yet wholly in character but with derby hats on their heads, worked as a team while they grappled with the problems of an aching tooth and laughing gas (*Leave 'Em Laughing*). For *The Finishing Touch* (1928) the behind-the-camera team was again Roach/McCarey/Stevens/Bruckman (not forgetting H. M. Walker, whose title cards set scenes so well that opening titles were retained after the move into talkies). The Boys were by now firmly established in their familiar guise, albeit here lightly disguised with overalls as they went about their work as jobbing builders. Hired to finish off a half-built house, they certainly do. By the time they are through the house is well and truly finished off. The film's culminating tit-for-tat sequence (another of the pair's growing arsenal of routines) ended in a brick- and rock-hurling exchange. The final rock the Boys hurl (after fighting one another for the privilege) is the one that has been preventing their truck from rolling down the hill – at the bottom of which stand the remains of their customer's house . . .

In *From Soup to Nuts* (1928) they are hired by Mrs Culpepper (Anita Garvin) to help out at what is intended to be a classy dinner party. Splashing soup, a strategically placed banana skin in Ollie's path as he carries in a giant cake, Stan's misunderstanding of what it means to serve salad without dressing – such lunacy soon puts paid to any class Mrs Culpepper's dinner party might have had.

You're Darn Tootin' (1928) falls into three distinct sections. It opens with the Boys working as bandsmen in an orchestra playing in a miniature version of the Hollywood Bowl. The conductor (Otto Lederer) becomes progressively more outraged at the incompetence of his clarinettist (Stan) and French horn-player (Ollie), whose

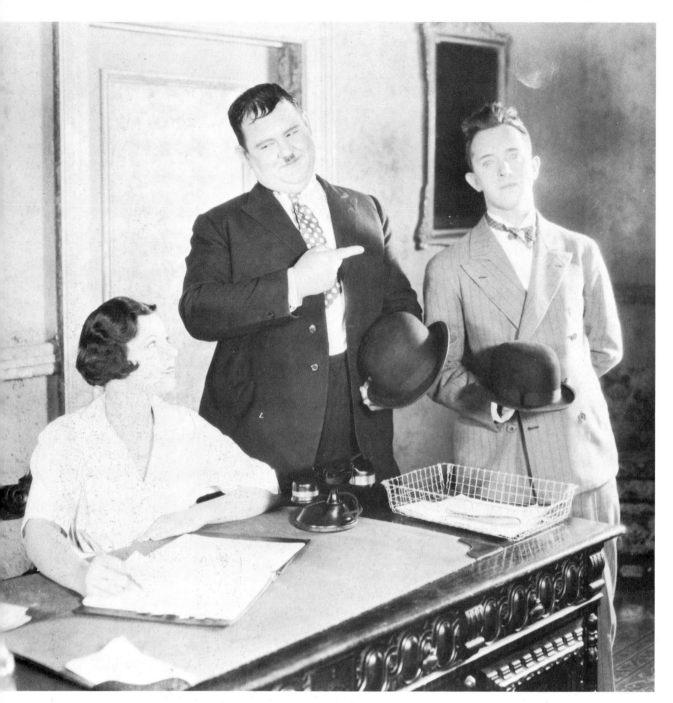

Guess which one is seeing the dentist in Leave 'Em Laughing.

With Edgar Kennedy in Leave 'Em Laughing.

Blissfully unaware . . .

. . . builders in The Finishing Touch.

Banging the drum for You're Darn Tootin'.

How come you still have your pants on? (You're Darn Tootin').

disruption of their concert ends with Stan knocking over a music stand, which in turn sends all the other stands flying, domino-like.

Fired, the Boys hand in their bandsmen's caps and return to their lodgings, where they are already many weeks behind with the rent. Tucking into what might well turn out to be their last meal for some time, Stan attempts to put salt in his soup but leaves the cap of the shaker loose. Ollie inevitably dumps the entire contents of the shaker in his soup and irritably exchanges his bowl for Stan's. Stan has meanwhile been performing with the pepperpot. The contents of the pepperpot end up in the soup, after which the merest movement of Stan's hand towards the ketchup bottle is enough to galvanize Ollie into pre-emptive action.

On their way to earn a crust from some street-corner busking, the Boys fall foul of a perennial hazard: the uncovered manhole. First Stan disappears down one in the middle of the road; later, as they stride confidently along the pavement, it is Ollie's turn. The frustration of their attempts to play their instruments leads to their squabbling and scrapping until they bad-temperedly destroy one another's instruments.

At dinner in Their Purple Moment.

They now turn on one another, punching and kicking; a stranger appears, asks what is going on and joins in. Gradually, others appear and join the fray in an orgy of shin-kicking and pants-pulling which leaves half the town bruised and trouser-less. Stan and Ollie make their exit inside one pair of pants pulled from a (very) fat man.

By now, while still imperfect, most of the screen vocabulary of Laurel and Hardy was in use. Ollie's resigned look into the camera, carefully controlled during editing by Stan, and Stan's bewildered head-scratching and habit of weeping when things became too much for him are just some of their ways. Most striking was the marked change in pace of Stan's work. The manic energy he had displayed in *Putting Pants on Philip* had

vanished, to be replaced by the measured tread of an increasingly somnolent dimwit.

The dimwit had wife trouble in *Their Purple Moment* (1928), while it was Ollie's turn to endure marital oppression in *Should Married Men Go Home?* (1928), in which Edgar Kennedy made one of his frequent appearances as victim of the Boys' excesses. A shift in the team's swiftly gelling relationship occurs in *Early to Bed* (1928), in which Ollie, after inheriting a fortune, uses his new-found power to dominate Stan. When Stan tires of this he decides to leave, accidentally breaks something and thereby discovers that he too has power, which he can exercise by systematically wrecking Ollie's expensive belongings.

Stan and Ollie were back playing a more

A scene sadly unused in Their Purple Moment.

recognizable version of themselves, though dressed in uniform, for *Two Tars* (1928). This film was one of the first of the Boys' to be directed by James Parrott (comedian Charley Chase's brother), who would go on to direct many of their best efforts. Parrott had worked as an actor in silent comedies, when he used the name Paul Parrott.

In *Two Tars* the Boys, on shore leave, rent a car. With Stan at the wheel they narrowly miss a pedestrian leaning against a pole. Dismissing his dim shipmate from the driving seat, Ollie takes over and explains that the first rule of the road is to keep one's eyes on it. To emphasize the point he looks at Stan and promptly drives into a lamp-post. 'What's rule number two?' Stan asks.

Before Ollie can answer, the lamp topples off the post and lands on his head. After surviving a minor skirmish with a recalcitrant chewing-gum machine, the Boys take two girls for a spin in the country only to find themselves in a traffic jam.

What happens next is a scene which gloriously demonstrates the comic potential of their tit-for-tat method of dealing with trouble. This time the extremes to which they go can best be described by the phrase coined by John McCabe in conversation with Stan Laurel: reciprocal destruction.

It all begins when Ollie tries to edge their car out of the traffic jam and is accidentally hit by another car, driven by Edgar Kennedy. Ollie gives Edgar's car a shunt, which damages the car behind *his*. Edgar assaults the two tars' car and

Ollie lording it over Stan in Early to Bed.

has his headlights ripped off for his effrontery. One of the headlights smashes the windscreen of another car, which brings another motorist into the act. As destruction and mayhem spreads through the jammed traffic a radiator is punctured, Stan is hit by a tomato, grease guns are fired, balloons are popped, the bags and baggage of one traveller are dumped repeatedly into the roadway, hats are crushed and, one by one, all the vehicles, drivers and passengers in the impatiently waiting queue are involved in the ensuing mass destruction. When a motorcycle cop is unwise enough to become involved, his bike is run over. He orders all the other motorists to follow Stan and Ollie as they make their escape. Taking the cop's instruction literally, they follow the Boys over the fields and into a railway tunnel. As a train enters the other end, all the cars back hastily out but the two tars, their car squashed to half its original width, get through.

Much less destructive, but ultimately as dangerous for the Boys, is *Habeas Corpus* (1928), in which they are hired by a mad professor to steal a body from a graveyard. Unaware that the police have been alerted to their loony employer's nefarious antics, Stan and Ollie head for the cemetery. When they lose their way, Ollie imperiously rejects Stan's offer to climb a signpost. At the top, Ollie reads the sign: 'Wet Paint', and comes down decidedly miffed and severely marked by his misadventure. Eventually arriving at the boneyard, the Boys hoist a body out of an open grave, unaware that this is a detective who is after the professor. With the 'body' in a sack over Stan's

Preparing for a spin in the country and . . .

. . . the first steps on a trail of destruction in Two Tars.

shoulder – which becomes unexpectedly lighter when the detective obligingly pops his feet out and walks along behind – they head back to town and the inevitable fearful panic when the dead man comes back to life.

In *We Faw Down* (1928) the Boys are married men who scheme their way out of their wives' reach in order to enjoy a game of poker. They succeed in getting out of the house despite the suspicions of their better halves. Ostensibly going to visit the theatre, they head for the card school but are innocently sidetracked into the apartment of two girls. They are spotted by their wives, who later watch ominously as Ollie describes the acts they claim to have seen. In this he is misguided by Stan's mimes of the theatre routines culled from a programme in the newspaper. Then Stan reads the headline. The theatre burned down! When one of the girls arrives with Ollie's waistcoat, the Boys take to their heels as Mrs Hardy reaches for a shotgun. As they race away, she lets fly and the explosion causes the rapid exit from all the adjoining apartments of several partially undressed erring husbands.

For *Liberty* (1929) Stan and Ollie are back in prison but quickly make a break for it. Picked up by friends who have brought clothes, they dress too hastily and manage to put on the wrong trousers. While Stan has on the biggest pair of pants a crab falls from a box at the fish market and finds a hiding place in the capacious seat, where it remains undetected. Later, after several embarrassingly unsuccessful attempts, they manage to swap trousers and when Ollie inserts his considerably bulkier posterior the crab is understandably irritated. By this time, the Boys' search for a private corner where they can exchange garments has led them to the top of a partly-built skyscraper – not the best of places for Ollie to discover he has a crabby crustacean where his shorts should be.

In *Liberty* many of the regulars are present: Leo McCarey directs from his own story, George Stevens is again the cameraman and James Finlayson is in the cast, as are regular bit-players Harry Bernard and Sam Lufkin. There is also an attractive young newcomer named Jean Harlow, who was to pop up in two other Laurel and Hardy films (*Double Whoopee* and *Bacon Grabbers*) before going on to stardom herself.

By now the silents were ceasing to be exactly that. So far, the Boys' films were content merely to employ synchronized sound effects and music for those theatres with the equipment and managerial desire to take advantage of the advances being made in Hollywood. In so doing their inventive use of sound which really makes an effect paved the way for what later became standard practice in films. The echoing 'boinggg!' of a frying-pan striking an unsuspecting head is only one of many devices Laurel and Hardy used at this time and, indeed, may well have originated.

However, for the ever-growing audience, eager to see the latest Laurel and Hardy adventure, sound did not matter very much, if at all. The silent comedy had become an established tradition in the world of popular entertainment and many seemed happy for it to remain as it had always been.

Mistaken identity, long a theme with comic potential, was at the core of *Wrong Again* (1929). This time Stan and Ollie, working at a stable, hear that the famous 'Blue Boy' has been stolen. A huge reward is offered for its return. As they have just been sweeping out the stall of a horse called 'Blue Boy', the Boys think they have it made. Of course, they have got it wrong again: the stolen 'Blue Boy' is the Gainsborough painting. Unaware that they are as far off-course as it is possible to be they take the horse to the 'owner's' mansion and announce they have 'Blue Boy'. The owner, upstairs and out of sight, is delighted and tells them to put it on the piano.

Surprised, but eager to please the owner from whom they confidently expect to collect the reward, Stan and Ollie gamely tackle the problem of getting the horse on to the piano. They eventually succeed, just before the police arrive with the stolen painting. Understandably indignant at the sight of a horse on his piano, the owner chases the Boys away with a shotgun and in the fracas the painting is ruined.

In *Wrong Again* the Boys' hats are used as comic props. For Stan, losing his hat is a matter of great consequence and one to which he applies what little concentration he can muster. The fact that every time he loses his hat and has to retrieve it he leaves Ollie smarting and fuming alone under the weight of the piano is, to him, beside the point. Capable only of grasping one thing at a time, Stan's screen persona has a sense of priorities as serenely certain as a child's.

Less tangible is the surrealistic image of a horse

Oops! and . . .

. . . Oops! again in Liberty.

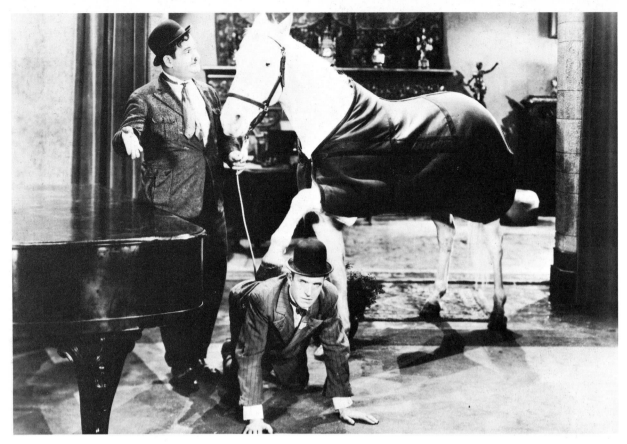

Gamely tackling the problem of getting a horse on to the piano in Wrong Again.

on a piano. Coming as it did between Luis Buñuel's *Un Chien andalou* (1928) and *L'Age d'or* (1930), with their strange vision of the world including a cow on a sofa, *Wrong Again* leaves an impression of a deeper intention behind the Boys' cockeyed clowning.

In *That's My Wife* (1929) Stan is called upon to impersonate Ollie's wife in order to fool a visiting relative who plans to hand over a large sum of money to what he fondly believes to be his happily married relatives. As the real Mrs Hardy has left home in protest against Stan's permanent residence in the spare room, Ollie persuades his reluctant pal to dress up in his wife's best gown and a wig borrowed from a doll. For a while this unlikely masquerade convinces the uncle that all is well, but a visit to a swanky restaurant ends in disastrous disarray after a conflict with a jewel thief and a drunk.

Conflict of a different sort provides the theme for *Big Business* (1929), in which the calm destruction of property, regularly touched upon in the

Boys' work, notably in *Two Tars*, reaches its apogee.

For this two-reeler there was a change of director. James W. Horne, who specialized in serials in the earliest years of Hollywood (and later returned to the genre in the late 1930s and early 1940s), joined the regular Roach/McCarey/Stevens/Walker team to create a supreme example of logical insanity.

This time Stan and Ollie are Christmas-tree salesmen, not achieving much success. At one house the irritated occupant, played by James Finlayson, slams the door on the tip of their sample tree. At their second ring Fin opens the door, but Stan is not quick enough and the tree is caught again. At a third attempt Stan triumphantly removes the tree just before Fin slams it shut again, but on this occasion the hapless salesman's coat is caught. Another ring at the bell brings back Fin, Stan releases his coat and tries once more to sell Fin a tree. This time Fin hurls the tree away. Then Stan decides to try to sell Fin a

An unwelcome guest and . . .

. . . an unlikely one in That's My Wife.

All friends with James Finlayson and Tiny Sandford in Big Business.

tree for the following Christmas. Mistakenly believing he has made a sale, Stan calls Ollie back – but Fin emerges, armed with clippers, and cuts the tree into little pieces.

Stan now takes out his pocket-knife, cuts off the house number and hacks a piece off the door frame. Fin tries to hit Stan but Ollie now takes a hand, prevents the assault on his pal and borrows Stan's knife to trim a few stray hairs from the house-owner's balding head. As the destruction escalates, Ollie's watch is smashed, Fin's doorbell is torn out and, when Fin attempts to call the police, Stan cuts the telephone wire and throws the instrument away. A tie is snipped, Fin cuts Ollie's shirt and Stan sprays Fin with water from his own hosepipe. The Boys then return to their car and prepare to leave. Fin, however, is just warming to the battle: he rips a headlamp from the Boys' car, they climb out to watch, and he promptly lets fly with the headlamp through the windscreen.

Having drawn a crowd, the Boys prepare to put on a real show. Topcoats off, they hurl a lamp through the window of Fin's house. He wrenches a door off their car. After Fin's progress has twice been hindered by a small tree on his front lawn Stan obligingly yanks it out of the ground. Stan and Ollie smash down Fin's front door and as his partner lobs out vases and *objets d'art*, Ollie swats them into smithereens with a spade. Calming down just a little, Ollie tries to stop Stan from wrecking Fin's piano. Then they both watch as Fin destroys all the trees in their car.

By now the car is a heap of metal and the house looks as if a bomb has hit it. During all this a cop (Tiny Sandford) has arrived but stays warily in his car waiting for something to happen against which he can take official action. Eventually, with the Boys' car in flames everyone calms down, they all shake hands and Fin is offered a placatory cigar. Unable to resist the humour of the situation, the Boys laugh and are chased away by the

Spluttering pens are just one of life's hazards (Double Whoopee).

cop. As they disappear down the street Fin settles down to his cigar, which promptly explodes.

Later, Hal Roach would recall that due to a misunderstanding the film crew allowed the Boys to wreck the wrong house but this appears to have been a slight case of publicity-minded lily-gilding. The house belonged to an employee who was well rewarded for any inconvenience the destruction might have caused him.

Rightly, the film has long been one of the established favourites of Laurel and Hardy fans. In its timing and above all in the amiably co-operative manner in which each player takes his turn before committing the next atrocity, it is impossible to think of any way in which *Big Business* could be improved. Certainly spoken dialogue would not have helped, indeed words would have proved a marked disadvantage in this purely visual sustained comic sequence.

In *Double Whoopee* (1929) the Boys are momentarily mistaken for visiting dignitaries and are greeted effusively by the manager of a swanky hotel – until he discovers that they are the new doorman and footman. Storylines had become relatively unimportant to the makers of Laurel and Hardy films and although some retained a narrative others did not. For the most part *Double Whoopee* is content to be a string of well devised and executed sight gags, one of which involves ripping off the back of a dress worn by a shapely blonde (Jean Harlow once again).

In *Bacon Grabbers* (1929) the pair are hired to collect goods from people who have fallen behind with their instalment payments, and in particular a radio from a noted hard man (Edgar Kennedy). Their efforts are almost the death of both themselves and Kennedy's character, but eventually they recover the radio. A passing steamroller delights Edgar by flattening the repossessed radio, but then his wife (played by Jean Harlow) announces that she has just paid for it. This time it is the Boys' turn to laugh – just as the steadily advancing steamroller flattens their car.

The Boys attract an unwanted pet in *Angora Love* (1929). Taking the animal, a goat that will not leave them alone, back to their hotel, they are forced to conceal it from the landlord (another Edgar Kennedy role). Part of their scheme involves eliminating the goat's unmistakable odour by bathing it, an act which makes concealment from Edgar even less likely to succeed.

The last three films were not released right away; they were temporarily withheld while the studio rushed out the Boys' first dialogue picture.

In the Boys' private lives there was, for the moment, some semblance of stability in their marriages. Yet both were embarked upon long-running affairs with other women. Fortunately for their public image they were able to offer to the nosey-parker world of Hollywood a front of relative propriety.

Stan and Lois lived comfortably and well, although he never appeared to need or want the ostentatious appurtenances of fame beloved of many Hollywood stars. Unfortunately the intense pressure at which Stan worked and his habits of relaxation, including heavy social drinking, raised problems which were allowed to fester under an apparently calm surface. There were rumours of affairs, including one which Fred Guiles suggests lasted for many years but did not culminate in marriage. For once, Stan's inclination to marry the women in his life was thwarted, in this instance because the lady was perfectly happy to remain unattached.

Babe's affair with Viola Morse was more open than Stan's but failed to come to the attention of that element of the press which revelled in such matters. It was probably as well, for however difficult life was for Lois Laurel it was not as bad as Myrtle Hardy's. She had struggled with Babe during the days before his career took off, survived his love for gambling but found that the combination of his flaws and the appearance of Viola too much. She began to drink heavily and became an alcoholic.

As the decade drew to a close the makers of silent movies were increasingly faced with the task of responding to the challenge of the talkies, the techniques and sound qualities of which had rapidly improved. The need for actors to cluster unconvincingly around a static microphone was a problem that had been quickly overcome, so it was no longer justifiable to dismiss sound as an element that was impossible to incorporate into a fast-paced comedy. Additionally, the spread of movie theatres capable of playing talkies to an audience more eager than ever to see *and* hear their favourite stars was a factor moviemakers ignored at their financial peril.

Already, following the public reaction to the songs and few spoken words in *The Jazz Singer*, genuinely all-talking movies had been made and released. Warner Brothers capitalized upon their lead with *Lights of New York* in 1928 and soon other studios were trying their hand. The synchronized disc pioneered by Vitaphone had severe limitations, unlike the rival sound-on-film systems which were also being developed. Before long, everyone was doing it – well, almost everyone, for there were a few who held out. Among the silent film comics the most obvious dissenter was Chaplin, who withstood the move to using dialogue until 1940.

Other great names of the silent era lapsed because their voices did not fit their previous screen personalities. Exotically glamorous ladies with accents redolent of the seamier streets of New York City could not retain their magic for audiences. In the case of John Gilbert it was not his voice, although this was the tale which was told for years (even to the extent of rumoured deliberate ruination by his enemies). Rather it was the inability of moviemakers to adjust quickly enough to the requirements for the spoken words to be scripted differently from those displayed on title cards. Although it took time to realize it, even the most fervent of lovers, such as those Gilbert portrayed, could not get away with speaking the kind of lines normally never encountered outside a Valentine card.

Just as entering talkies was a decision that troubled the leading stars of dramatic films, so it was a matter of considerable concern for Stan Laurel and Oliver Hardy. In the past two years they had become phenomenally successful. They themselves were not yet fully aware of just *how* popular they really were. They had some hints from their growing fan mail and both were aware that their pictures were popular, since Roach was able to book them without difficulty. And, of course, the studio happily kept on making new ones.

The Boys therefore had no more desire than anyone else to change a winning formula. Apart from the seeming folly of tampering with success, neither was at an age, nor a career stage, for change to be undertaken lightly. At the end of 1929 Ollie was fast approaching his 38th birthday, while Stan would be 40 in a few months' time. Ollie had been a movie actor for 15 years while Stan's stage career had begun more than 20 years previously.

Making a career shift at this point in their lives was not an easy decision. But the change had to be made, and it duly was.

Avoiding getting the goat in Angora Love.

Taking the strain off the train in Berth Marks.

CHAPTER FIVE

Unaccustomed As We Are

The Classic Talkies

'You know, Ollie, I've been thinking.'

Stan Laurel

Despite the drawbacks of the synchronized disc method of teaming sound with moving pictures, even the detractors were forced to concede that the principal of talking pictures was here to stay.

The Boys' first talkie was the appropriately titled *Unaccustomed As We Are* (1929), and while it might not be one of their best efforts it demonstrated two important points: one was that the makers of the Laurel and Hardy films were not about to let the coming of sound divert them into gimmickry or any serious change in direction or style; the other was that the Boys' voices perfectly complemented their appearance and personas.

Stan's voice, with its deliberate, slightly pedantic delivery and faintly alien (to American ears) accent fitted his screen character perfectly. Babe's voice was a similarly perfect vehicle for his unctuously polite turn of phrase when addressing the ladies or passing policemen, yet was capable of a frustrated edginess when turned on to the hapless Stan. The orotund Southern gentleman's speech patterns admirably suited his on-screen cloak of would-be gentility.

Although slight in plot, *Unaccustomed As We Are* showed that the use of sound effects, with which they had already experimented, could be a regular and well-used attribute. Their dialogue, which was sparingly used, suited the characters and the plot without becoming a means of developing either. In essence, the talking Laurel and Hardy films were silents with a garnish of sound and dialogue. They did not depend upon it.

The cast of *Unaccustomed As We Are* included Edgar Kennedy and Mae Busch, who appeared as Mrs Hardy, a role she would develop into a way of life and which would earn her an unusual immortality. Also featured was Thelma Todd, who was soon to be the star of a highly popular series of comedies before her early death in 1935.

Berth Marks (1929) puts the Boys on a train bound for Pottsville, where they are due to appear at the local vaudeville theatre. What their act is like is anyone's guess but it is unlikely to have rivalled the effect of their passage through the train. Leaving chaos in their wake, they retire for the night to the sleeping car, where, instead of using the washroom in which to disrobe, as would any normal traveller, they prepare for bed in the cramped space of a single berth. Their strenuous efforts eventually succeeding, they settle down to rest only to learn that the train has reached Pottsville. They leave hastily, clad only in longjohns and derbies, while on board the train the rest of the passengers continue the fighting the Boys innocently began.

In *Men o'War* (1929) Stan and Ollie, this time back in the navy, meet two girls in the park. After an embarrassing misunderstanding when Ollie finds a pair of ladies' bloomers while the girl is looking for a pair of lost gloves, they become friendly. Ignoring their white sailor suits, one girl declares, 'Oh, I just love soldiers.' 'Meet the general,' Ollie says, indicating his shipmate. The Boys take the girls for a soda, a dangerous move given that they have only 15 cents to spend. Stan's inability to grasp the fact that he is supposed to say 'No' when asked if he wants a drink lands them with a bill they can't pay. Ollie departs with the girls leaving Stan to the mercy of the soda-jerk

Jerks at the soda fountain in Men o'War.

(James Finlayson). For once inspired, Stan gambles on a slot-machine, wins the jackpot, and they can move happily on to the rest of their afternoon's entertainment. When they take the girls rowing on the lake, the Boys' efforts with the oars prove disastrous: they row frantically round in circles until Ollie declares, 'Give me that oar. I'll have to take charge of this.' All attempts to steer a trouble-free course fail miserably as other boats are knocked and swamped. As everyone scrambles into their boat and a pillow fight breaks out, Finlayson's character, who is also the owner of the boats, grows steadily more and more agitated (no one could display agitation quite as startlingly as Fin). Eventually, with the aid of a passing policeman, Fin rows out to join the fray only to prove

the final straw. The boat sinks and everyone ends up in the water.

Perfect Day (1929) was intended to be a story about a day out in the country, but as cast and crew explored the problems surrounding the seemingly simple venture of a family setting out for a picnic the movie became instead a perfectly executed stationary saga in which no one gets anywhere.

Stan and Ollie and their wives are preparing for the excursion by making sandwiches, but as there is a swing door between the living room and the kitchen mishaps inevitably occur. Also due to go on the picnic is their uncle (played by Edgar Kennedy), whose well-bandaged gouty foot is clearly destined to be the object of later disaster.

Men o'War.

Finally making it to the car, everyone climbs aboard and calls goodbye to the neighbours. Ollie prepares to drive off. An instantaneous puncture holds up departure and the Boys' attempts to change the wheel result in a series of accidents to Edgar's foot, each more excruciatingly painful than the last. With the wheel changed they call their goodbyes once more and Ollie revs up the engine. Unfortunately, Stan has forgotten to remove the jack and the wheels spin fruitlessly. When the jack is lowered the car lists alarmingly – the spare, too, is flat.

Understandably irritated by all this, Ollie hurls the jack away – straight through a neighbour's window. Back it comes, through the windscreen, which prompts a brick from Stan through another window. This results in a brick being thrown through a window of the Boys' house. The appearance of the parson puts a stop to the scrap and once more everyone clambers aboard the car and yells their goodbyes. Now the car will not start; another attempt causes the engine to go up in smoke. With the fire eventually out more goodbyes are said and this time the car moves off, turns the corner triumphantly and promptly sinks out of sight into one of those impossibly deep mud-filled holes that lie in wait for the unwary throughout the world of Laurel and Hardy.

The Boys are back in prison for *The Hoose-Gow* (1929), although unlike their situation in *The Second Hundred Years* this time they are there by mistake. This is just one sign of how the Roach

Heading for The Hoose-Gow.

With Edgar Kennedy but . . .

. . . without their dignity in Night Owls.

Unfolding domestic havoc in Brats.

studio had developed their characters in accordance with audience perceptions. Stan and Ollie were now innocents abroad in a world which regularly did them grave injustice.

After futilely attempting to escape, the Boys settle into the routine of the prison and, not surprisingly, manage to disrupt everything and everyone from governor (James Finlayson) to inmates. While their behaviour naturally fails to endear them to the warden (Tiny Sandford), the governor is particularly displeased when they wreck his car by trying to block a hole in its radiator with rice. When everyone is covered in gobs of boiled rice the governor finally drives off only to hit a paint truck. The Boys, hoping to escape in the governor's car, end up covered in paint – and still in prison.

The international appeal of the Laurel and Hardy films was growing and many of their movies at this time were made in multiple versions with foreign-language soundtracks. Although this cost more than dubbing it had the distinct advantage of allowing foreign audiences to hear the Boys' real voices: they read their lines phonetically from cue cards. The same procedure was followed by other members of the cast although in some instances, especially for the leading ladies, foreign actresses were brought in. For example, Georgette Rhodes replaces Anita Garvin in the French version of *Blotto* (1930), while her place is taken by Linda Loredo for the Spanish market. In some cases alternative scenes were shot, and the resulting films therefore differ from one version to another.

Recently, Mark Lipson of Hal Roach Studios discovered six Laurel and Hardy films in the MGM archives. He told Richard Bann, who promptly realized that these were foreign-

Well Below Zero.

language versions of *Blotto, Chickens Come Home, Night Owls, Below Zero, Be Big* and *The Laurel and Hardy Murder Case*. The reporter of this discovery for *American Film*, October 1986, observes that certain sequences in the films (which have now been carefully copied, frame by frame) are a shade spicier that would have been thought appropriate for home consumption in 1930s America. Of course, 'spicy' for Laurel and Hardy is still decidedly circumspect.

Although foreign-language versions were made of *Brats* (1930), there was no need for cast changes as all four parts are played by the Boys. Stan and Ollie play not only themselves but the roles of their own sons. Using interesting if unconvincing double exposure and a larger-than-life set, a story of domestic havoc is unfolded, setting their adult and child-like selves against the similarly child-like but 'real' children.

In *Below Zero* (1930) Stan and Ollie are down on their luck, as usual. Attempts to wring a few cents from the public by busking fail miserably. At first the problem is the fact that they are singing and playing outside a deaf and dumb institute, but later their lack of aptitude for their task makes itself felt. One lady enquires politely how much they expect to make on the average street. When told '50 cents', she tosses them a dollar and invites them to move on two streets. A very tall woman (Blanche Payson) appears carrying a pail. She takes a dislike to the pair's efforts and washes Ollie's face with snow, in retaliation for which Stan throws her pail away. Not in the least deterred by this, she smashes Ollie's double-bass over his head, then throws Stan's harmonium into the roadway. The inevitable passing truck crushes it to matchwood.

Flat broke, they drift miserably away. Then

Two men about town.

they find a well-filled wallet and celebrate with steak dinners for themselves and the policeman who saves them from a tough guy with his own plans for the money. Ollie's attempts to impress their guest and the waiter (Tiny Sandford) with his knowledge of restaurant etiquette fall foul of Stan's unwitting sabotage.

'Oh, *garçon*,' Ollie calls after the waiter.

'Yes, sir?'

'Bring me a *parfait.*'

'Yes, sir.'

'Put one on my steak, too,' Stan chimes in.

'You don't put *parfaits* on steaks,' Ollie says disgustedly. 'Just cancel the *parfaits.*'

'Yes, sir.'

'But bring me a small *demi-tasse.*'

'Yes, sir.'

'Oh, Gaston,' Stan calls.

'Yes, sir?'

'Bring me one too, in a big cup.'

Ollie glares at his companion. 'A big cup! Where were you brung up? Pass the *hors d'oeuvres.*' He beams at the policeman. 'You'll pardon my friend's ignorance,' he adds, before crunching noisily into a celery stalk.

Many of the films the Boys made at this time were directed by James Parrott with storylines by Leo McCarey and H. M. Walker, who had graduated from title-card writer to dialogue writer. Although now fully geared to talkies, the Roach studios wisely retained the opening title card, which often set up the following film with a sharply perceptive comment.

Parrott's early work as an actor in his own series of comedies and his direction of some Laurel and Hardy films shows a high standard of ability. *Two Tars* and *Perfect Day* are two of his earlier efforts, while those on which he was now launched were of an equal, if not higher, standard. Indeed, the peak of his work with the team was to result in an Oscar for *The Music Box*.

In *Hog Wild* (1930) the Boys fully hit their stride, producing the first talkie that was at least as good as the best of their silents. Ollie and his wife (Fay Holderness) are on mildly warring terms (the film's opening sequence in which Ollie searches for his hat – which is on his head – features many resigned camera looks from them both). In an attempt to placate her, Ollie agrees to fit a new radio aerial to the roof of his house. In this endeavour he is joined by Stan, with predictable results. The very predictability of much of the Boys' work was a splendidly used asset. Owing to this technique audiences begin laughing long before the gag, continue laughing *at* the gag (which never suffers but is usually enhanced by the build-up) and then continue laughing afterwards, partly because it was funny but also because they have been proved right in their expectations.

This film also demonstrates another comedy technique the Boys used as well as anyone: the repeated gag. Once on the roof of Ollie's little house, Stan contrives to leave a pole lying where Ollie can step on it. Seconds later Ollie has fallen off the roof and into the decorative lily pond in the garden beneath. Back on the roof, Ollie is tumbled off again by Stan's misuse of the aerial wire. Determined there will be no repeat, Ollie ropes himself to the chimney, but when Stan clambers on to his back their combined weight is too much. This time they fall off together and take the chimney with them. With Stan safely in the house, Ollie ventures roofwards once more. This time Stan manages to administer an electric shock and Ollie falls through the hole left by the chimney.

Unusually for a Laurel and Hardy film, *Hog Wild* also includes a sequence that would not have been out of place in a Mack Sennett slapstick comedy. Making a final assault on the roof, Ollie clambers up the ladder which is propped into the back seat of Stan's car. As Ollie reaches the top of the ladder Stan accidentally starts the car moving and a hair-raising race through the streets follows.

During this same year, 1930, Laurel and Hardy made the first of only two known colour movies (the second was a short film for the Department of Agriculture made during World War II), but *Rogue Song*, which starred opera singer Lawrence Tibbett, became one of Hollywood's lost treasures. In the late 1970s a copy of the soundtrack was discovered and a little later a short sequence of film was found. This depicts a storm during which Stan and Ollie (in their roles of Ali-Bek and Murza-Bek) take refuge in a very dark cave, in which each is curious to know where the other has acquired a fur coat. The answer is that neither is wearing fur, the cave is a bear's den.

Also longer than their customary two-reelers was the three-reel *Laurel and Hardy Murder Case* (1930), which opens with the Boys fishing for their supper on the dockside. Ollie reads an item in a newspaper about a will from which he thinks

Lost! The Rogue Song.

The Laurel and Hardy Murder Case.

Going Hog Wild.

Fishing for their supper in The Laurel and Hardy Murder Case.

James Finlayson big-game hunting in Another Fine Mess.

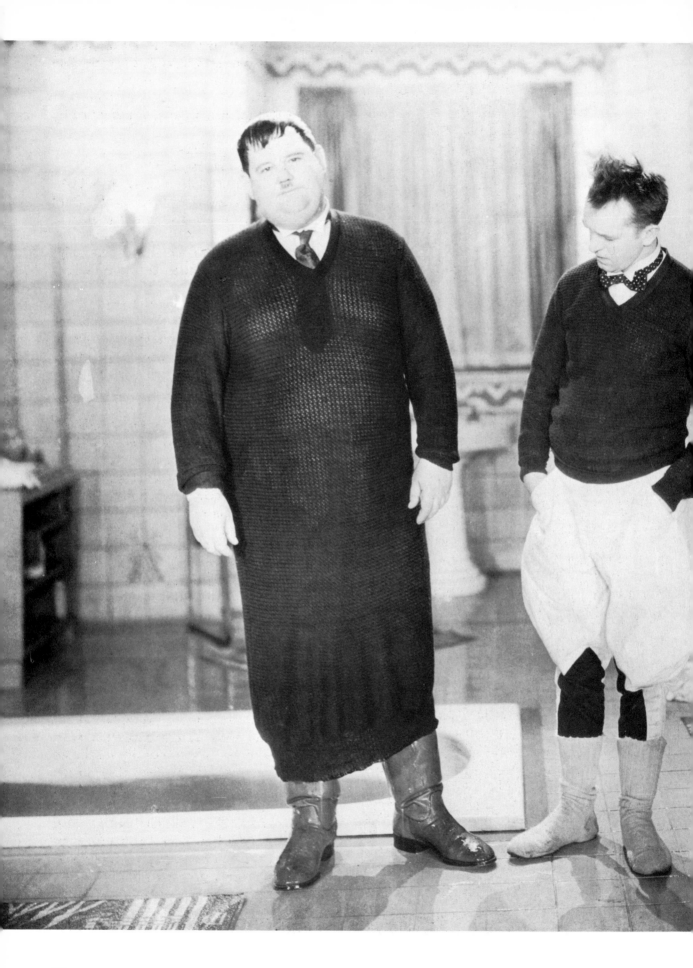

they would benefit. But Stan is not too certain about his antecedents when Ollie quizzes him about an uncle.

'Is he living?'

'No, he fell through a trapdoor and broke his neck.'

'Was he building a house?'

'No, they were hanging him.'

When told that the inheritance is $3 million, Stan's brain cannot conceive of such a sum. 'Three million dollars! Is that as much as a thousand?' he asks.

'Why, man alive, it's twice as much!' Ollie states in a woeful attempt to prove his superior intelligence.

This film leans heavily upon many of the standard 'old dark house' ploys for its laughs and does not have the by now expected, if tenuous, contact with reality. The ending, which reveals that the Boys have been dreaming it all, serves only to underline the film's unsatisfactory link with reality.

Although not always retained for TV and other screenings, several Laurel and Hardy films use inventive opening titles. A circular saw buzzes across the screen to wipe the credits in one, while windscreen wipers achieve a similar effect in another film. For *Another Fine Mess* (1930) the titles are spoken alternately by twin girls. In this film the Boys return to the insane logicality of their best work. Pursued by a policeman they have managed to offend, Stan and Ollie take refuge in a house whose owner (Finlayson) has gone abroad after advertising his house for rental. The butler and maid also leave but the Boys' potential hideaway is promptly invaded by a rich couple who hope to rent the vacant house. Ollie and Stan hastily disguise themselves as owner and butler respectively. But the real owner's advertisement stated that there was also a maid, so Stan has to double in drag. The eventual unexpected return of the real owner sends Stan and Ollie into hiding in the trophy room. From there they emerge dressed in an animal skin and are pursued by the cops. Out in the street and still dressed as something rather like a pantomime yak, they commandeer a tandem from a pair of passing cyclists and make their getaway. *Another Fine Mess* is, substantially, a re-working of their *Duck*

Fashion plates in Be Big.

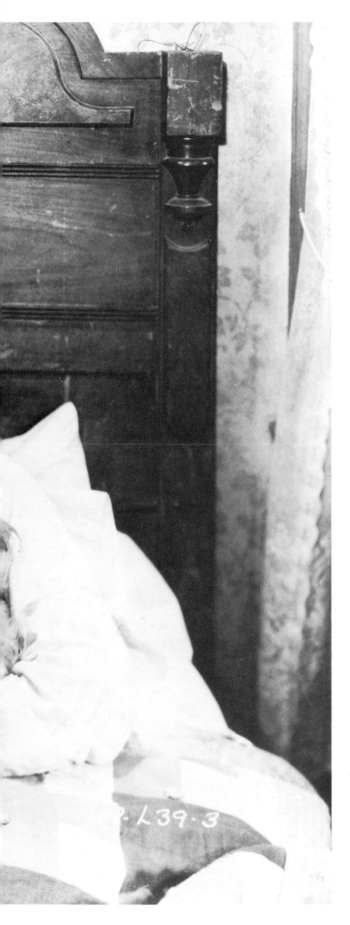

Soup, one example of many in which Laurel and Hardy re-used the substance of past successes. During this period of their career such re-makes and re-usage generally resulted in an improvement over the original.

The longer three-reel format continued with other successes, *Be Big* and *Chickens Come Home* (both 1931). In the former the principal gag, which is developed at far greater length than most lesser comics could have managed (or would even have dared), centres upon Stan's attempts to help Ollie take off a pair of riding boots. The boots, which are actually Stan's, are too tight and the struggle to remove them wrecks furniture and fittings before their wives (Anita Garvin and Isabelle Keith) return and express their disapproval with shotguns which blow the Boys and the wall-bed in which they are vainly hiding through the wall and into the street.

Chickens Come Home is a further example of the re-use of material. The original version of this was the 1927 *Love 'Em and Weep* in which James Finlayson, in his first film with the Boys, starred as Titus Tillsbury, whose domestic bliss is marred by the appearance at his home of a blackmailing old flame (Mae Busch). In that version Stan played his friend and Ollie was a house guest. In the re-make Ollie is the victim and Finlayson plays the butler while Stan and Mae Busch retain their original roles. Stan's attempts to dissuade the blackmailer develop into a minor furore as the agitated Mae searches his pockets while in the lobby of her apartment house, an action which reduces Stan to tearful hysteria. Worse is to come during a visit to Ollie's house where Mae briefly pretends to be Stan's wife. By this time Mrs Hardy (Thelma Todd) has become decidedly disenchanted with her husband's behaviour. When the real Mrs Laurel arrives Mrs Hardy chases her husband and his partner into the night.

Laughing Gravy (1931) is yet another re-make; this time the goat of *Angora Love* is replaced with a small dog but otherwise the story is left pretty much unchanged. Once again, the re-make improved upon the original, although the use of a rather endearing dog instead of a goat gave this film a touch more sanity. The Boys' concern for their pet is such that when landlord Charlie Hall

The Boys with 'Laughing Gravy'.

Yet another nice mess in Our Wife.

throws the dog out into the snow Ollie goes out to retrieve him. Accidentally locked out, Ollie eventually attracts Stan's attention and tells him to lower a rope made from knotted sheets. The dog is hauled up but Ollie's weight almost brings Stan through the window.

Our Wife (1931) has Ollie preparing to marry, but the would-be bride (Jean 'Babe' London) is obstructed by her father (Finlayson), who forbids the wedding. Determined to marry his beloved, Ollie decides that they will elope and asks Stan to come along and help. Unfortunately, he fails to check that Stan understands the meaning of the word 'elope', and as a result finds himself up against the equally determined Finlayson. Somehow surviving the predictable problems with a ladder (the bride-to-be is the physical counterpart of Ollie), they manage the elopement but the planned wedding ends up in total disarray thanks

to the inability of the Justice of the Peace (played by Ben Turpin, the owner of the most famous crossed eyes in movie history) to see straight.

The ancient and honourable tradition of parodying successful straight movies (so well-developed by Stan in his early film career) was revived for *Pardon Us* (1931), inspired by *The Big House* (1930), in which Wallace Beery and Chester Morris had starred.

In *Pardon Us* the Boys are sent to prison for bootlegging. Prohibition was no crime in the eyes of the majority in America, so the Boys' failure to observe it maintained their new role as sympathetic, if dunderheaded, characters. Once behind the walls Stan and Ollie quickly get off on the wrong foot thanks to Stan's bad tooth, which causes him to emit impolite raspberries at decidedly inconvenient moments.

The Boys are destined to share a cell with the

Frozen stiff in Laughing Gravy.

Preparing to bootleg the booze that will put them . . .   *. . . in prison with Walter Long in* Pardon Us.

prison's toughest and most feared inmate, Tiger (Walter Long), and to attend education classes conducted by James Finlayson's character, in mortar board and gown. Unwittingly swept up into a Tiger-led escape bid, Stan and Ollie hide among a crowd of cotton-pickers. Hastily blacking-up (a practice not yet frowned upon in show business), the Boys join in with the field hands' singing of 'Lazy Moon', on which Ollie is especially effective. Eventually recaptured, Stan and Ollie find themselves once more unwilling participants in one of Tiger's prison breaks, which this time involves the use of guns. A machine-gun in Stan's hands predictably goes off prematurely, endangering the lives and limbs of everyone within spraying distance. With the weapon taking on a life of its own in the Boys' hands the prisoners are cowed into submission. A grateful warden pardons them, but not before Stan's raspberrying tooth almost undoes all their good work.

This film, which at just under an hour's running time is their first feature film, was also made in multiple languages, but the practice was soon to be abandoned on economic grounds.

Pardon Us proved that the Boys' comedy could sustain more than the two-reelers which still make up the bulk of their work. The fact that most of their later full-length feature films had marked failings suggests that somewhere along the line inadequate forethought was given to the stories and, above all, the roles that Stan and Ollie would play in them.

For now, as 1931 drew to a close, there were still good if unexceptional two-reelers to be made. *Come Clean* contains a good example of their ability to build comic dialogue through repetition of particular words and phrases. The Laurels visit the Hardys, arriving just too late for dinner. Mrs Hardy asks Stan if he would like anything.

'Well, I could go for a dish of ice cream.'

'We haven't got any ice cream,' Ollie says.

'Well, you could get some ice cream,' Stan retorts.

The hazards of preparing for dinner in Come Clean.

Another pie and . . .

. . . another collapsing roof in One Good Turn.

Ollie's wife agrees. 'Yes, dearie, you could get some ice cream.'

Disgruntled, Ollie says, 'Get me my new hat, dear, and I'll get some ice cream.'

'You going to get it in your hat?' Stan enquires.

'No, I'm not going to get it in my hat.'

At the ice-cream parlour progress deteriorates rapidly after Ollie has asked for a quart of ice cream.

'Yes, sir,' says the attendant. 'What flavour?'

'What flavours have you?'

'Strawberry, pineapple and vanilla.'

'What flavour do you want?' Ollie asks Stan.

'I'll have chocolate.'

'I'm sorry but we're out of chocolate.'

'Have you any mustachio?'

'No, we're out of mustachio.'

'They're out of mustachio,' Stan tells Ollie.

'Yes.'

'He's out of mustachio.'

'Mmm-mm.'

'What other flavours are you out of?' Stan asks innocently.

'Strawberry . . . we're out of orange, gooseberry and chocolate.'

'All right, I'll have it without chocolate.'

By now, Ollie has had enough. 'Didn't the gentleman just tell you that he didn't have any chocolate?'

'I just told the gentleman I didn't want . . .'

'Just give us a quart of any kind that's handy. Please.'

On the way back home the Boys save a suicidal Mae Busch from the river and then, typically innocent of real involvement with another woman, they have to conceal her from their wives.

In *One Good Turn* they try to help an old lady (Mary Carr) who is being harassed by the evil financier (Finlayson) who holds the mortgage on her home. Unfortunately the Boys, who make a determined effort to raise the money she needs, do not realize that the lady and Fin are members of the local drama group and were merely rehearsing their next play.

In *Beau Hunks*, a four-reeler, Ollie is preparing to marry but when he is jilted decides to join the Foreign Legion. With Stan in tow they arrive in the desert, where they find they are sharing a barrack room with several others jilted by the same girl (represented by a photograph of Jean Harlow). Beset by sandstorms and Riffs, the Boys survive being lost in the desert only to turn up, all two of them, as saviours of a besieged fort. They succeed in routing the barefoot Arabs with the aid of a box of tacks and capture the Riff chief (who also mourns over a picture of Jean).

During 1932 and 1933 the flow of Laurel and Hardy movies continued unabated, yet the Roach team was able to sustain a remarkably high standard.

In *Helpmates* (1932) Ollie takes advantage of his wife's absence to throw a party and is faced with clearing up the mess in time for her return. He calls Stan, who has missed the festivities, and enlists his help in concealing the evidence. While Stan carefully (and successfully) washes a huge

Pride of the Legion in Beau Hunks.

pile of dirty dishes Ollie tidies himself up in preparation for meeting his wife. Unfortunately, a carpet sweeper that has already laid Ollie low does the trick once more, this time sending him crashing into the pile of dishes. The collapse of the stove pipe and the subsequent soot-fall over Ollie is followed by his doomed attempt to wash but, blinded by the soot, Ollie picks up a slab of butter in mistake for soap.

Seeking a towel, Ollie opens a cupboard door and is covered in a cascade of flour. While he changes his clothes Stan continues his task, only to be foiled by a blocked-up wastepipe on the kitchen sink. When Ollie returns he watches as Stan tries to throw the water through the sash window, but the window falls, causing the water to splash back, narrowly missing Ollie. He goes

outside, reopens the window, props it up with a stick, then accidentally knocks a potted plant to the ground. He stoops to retrieve it, standing up just in time to receive the contents of Stan's washing-up bowl in his face. Angrily he hurls the plant at Stan, but it flies straight through the house and hits a neighbour who is watering his lawn with a hosepipe. The hose squirts in through another window of the Hardy house and greets Ollie with a total drenching when he enters that room in a desperate search for more clean clothes.

Ollie's attempt to dry his clothes in front of the stove ends up in predictable disaster when the gas is turned on before he has a match ready. With the suit destroyed in the ensuing explosion Ollie is reduced to wearing a uniform akin to that of an officer in the Ruritanian Navy (and almost as

When Ollie returns, eye blackened by his already irate spouse, he finds Stan in the midst of a roofless, wall-less house. The floor is not in good shape either: Ollie crashes through it. 'Well, I guess there's nothing else I can do,' Stan remarks. 'I guess not,' Ollie replies. Stan leaves after first being requested to close the door, about the only part of the house still standing. As Ollie sits in his armchair, exposed to the elements, it starts to rain. Ollie's brush with the fates ends as, carefully, and with dignified elegance, he flicks an invisible speck of dust from his pants.

The development of the sight gags and the rate at which they build one upon the other makes *Helpmates* an instructive example of the art of the silent moviemaker for, with the exception of Ollie's telephone conversations, with his wife and with Stan, little of what transpires acknowledges the coming of sound. The attempt by Stan to remove water from the blocked-up sink and the successive disasters is an example of the logical insanity of gag-progression.

The slow but inexorable build-up to disaster appeared again in *The Music Box* (1932), which was a re-make of the Boys' earlier *Hats Off* even to the extent of re-using the same flight of steps in

Welcome home! (Helpmates).

flamboyant as that he had worn in *Fortune's Mask*). He heads for the station to collect his wife, leaving Stan to tidy up. With the house spotless, Stan decides on a finishing touch and attempts to light a log-effect gas fire – with kerosene.

With Walter Long and Bobby Burns in Any Old Port.

Hollywood up which to haul the item they are delivering. This time, the item is a large packing case containing a player piano. After unloading the box from their horse-drawn cart, a task not made easier by the actions of their malevolent nag, they struggle part way up the steps only to be met by a nursemaid who insists on her right of way. Thanks largely to Ollie's gallantry, the box breaks loose and bounces down to the bottom of the steps, its contents jangling discordantly. The maid's glee is countered by Stan, who kicks her smartly in the seat. She reports this affront to a policeman ('He kicked me in the middle of my daily duties') who, when he reaches the scene, finds the Boys part way up the steps again. Called down by the law, the Boys neglect to secure the piano, and down it comes again. Their next effort to reach the top of the steps is almost stopped by the appearance of the blustering Professor Theodore von Schwarzenhoffen (Billy Gilbert), who is sent packing. With the piano finally at the top of the steps Ollie manages to fall in the swimming-pool. Finally at the door of the house, they let go of the piano, which promptly takes off back the way it came as the Boys chase hopelessly after it. Ollie catches hold but the impetus is too great and it drags him with it all the way to the bottom.

Time mercifully passes and the Boys have the piano back at the top only to be met by the postman (Charlie Hall), who enquires why they did not drive their horse and cart round by the road, which would have brought them up to the top. Once they have been shown the error of their ways the Boys do the logical thing – they take the piano back down again and load it on to the cart. With the piano at the house once more, this time the easy way, they find the owner is not at home and decide to lift the box in through an upper window. After several minor disasters which do nothing to improve the structure of the house, the Boys manage to bring the piano down to the ground floor just in time for the return of the owner – none other than Professor von Schwarzenhoffen, who, it seems, hates pianos. The arrival of his wife, who has bought the piano as a surprise present for him, changes his mind and he agrees to sign the delivery note. He uses Stan's pen, which covers him in ink, and the Boys take to their heels.

This is a movie which uses sound mostly to enhance sight gags. The main exception is the scene when the Boys switch on the player piano and engage in a delightful dance routine to the accompaniment of the patriotic songs which burst forth.

The Music Box won the Oscar as Best Live Action Comedy Short Subject of 1931–2. Nevertheless, with the minor exception of the dance scene, this was a film which drew its essence from the days of the silents.

Similarly reliant upon sight gags, although much less inventive, is *County Hospital* (1932), a splendidly anarchic romp through some well-signposted routines involving a heavily-plastered leg (Ollie's) and Stan's attempts to help its owner prepare to leave hospital. Though Ollie was not expecting to go home just yet, Stan's use of the weight that holds Ollie's leg in the air as a nutcracker causes minor mayhem, so the surgeon (Billy Gilbert) throws them out. Before leaving, Stan manages to sit on a hypodermic syringe. A nurse declares that the needle's contents will cause him to sleep for a month. With Ollie in his car, encased leg perched dangerously on top of the seat, Stan prepares to drive them home but falls asleep along the way. The resulting crash between two streetcars thoroughly wrecks the Boys' car which, bent at right-angles, circles endlessly.

Pack Up Your Troubles (1932) is not as densely packed with gags as the earlier feature, *Pardon Us*. The story centres upon the Boys' attempts to find the grandparents of a little girl whose father was their buddy in the war but who did not make it back home. The gags are there, but well spaced out along a relatively orthodox storyline. Perhaps a touch more perception might have shown that this was the wrong way for Laurel and Hardy to go: their continuing two-reelers proved, after all, that they were a long way from exhausting their capacity to raise laughs.

This capacity did not rely entirely upon visual humour. They could and did take advantage of sound for entertaining dialogue. A recurring device in the films had Stan come up with a genuinely bright idea, explain it succinctly and coherently to Ollie but then fail miserably when asked to repeat it.

In *Towed in a Hole* (1932) they are fish salesmen with ambitions, as Stan demonstrates to Ollie in between toots on a horn.

'You know, Ollie, I . . . I've been thinking.'

'What about?'

'I . . . know how we could make a lot more money.'

Heading for an Oscar
(The Music Box).

With Charles Gamora as
The Chimp.

Hard-boiled eggs and nuts! (County Hospital).

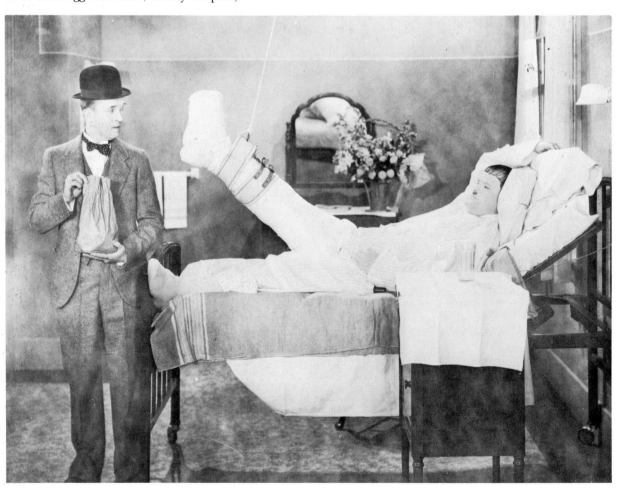

Vivien Oakland overcome with bootleg gin in 'Scram!'.

In the alley with Jacqui Lyn
(Pack Up Your Troubles, 1932).

'How?'

'Well, if . . . if we caught our own fish . . . we wouldn't have to pay for it. Then whoever we sold it to, it'd be clear profit.'

'Tell me that again.'

'Well, if you caught a fish, and whoever you sold it to they wouldn't have to pay for it. Then the profits would . . . they'd go to the fish if . . . if you . . .'

By this time, Stan's first, coherent, attempt has finally penetrated Ollie's obtuseness.

'I know exactly what you mean,' he says. 'Your idea is to eliminate the middleman.'

At which Stan, triumphantly relieved, nods his head emphatically and toots his horn.

'That's a pretty smart thought,' Ollie adds.

Of course, this dialogue is prelude to the customary and inexorable descent into a chaos of sight gags as the Boys buy and attempt to make seaworthy a fishing boat with which to put Stan's bright idea into practice.

In 1932 Stan and Babe had been working feverishly for five years and needed a rest. Eventually they decided to travel together to Europe, Stan to visit relatives in England, Babe to sample Scotland's golf courses. For the first time in many years they were outside Hollywood and exposed to an army of fans of which they were only vaguely aware. The mob scenes began in Chicago between trains and continued in New York. When their boat docked in Southampton the Boys were held on board ship by a hastily contrived excuse. Finally allowed ashore, they found a band playing and massed crowds whistling 'The Cuckoo Song' (a composition of Marvin Hatley's which had become a theme tune to be

The ever-popular Mae Busch proving not so . . . in Their First Mistake.

Oliver as man and wife in Twice Two.

Out of bowlers for Fra Diavolo.

played at the start of their movies). In London the wild enthusiasm was redoubled and the Boys began to realize that this would be no restful holiday. They were invited to make a record and also to broadcast on the BBC. Throughout the main provincial cities of England and in Glasgow their reception was the same. There was no escape in France, either, where they were driven through thronged Paris streets in the President's car.

It was an experience that opened their eyes and warmed their hearts. They had never imagined that they were so successful and popular, and quite clearly it had never crossed their minds that two Hollywood comedians could be the target of so much love.

When they returned to Hollywood, not especially rested but undoubtedly revitalized by their reception in Europe, it was to make yet more movies. In time there would be a marked shift in emphasis. For one thing they would make fewer films, and the days of the comedy short, which had provided the basis of their success, were

numbered. At least, this is what the studio thought as it decided to redirect their joint career. With hindsight it is possible to see that this was not the best thing to have happened. The unparalleled success the team enjoyed was founded in the short film. All of their best work had been in two-reelers, while the three-reeler allowed as much expansion as they needed. Feature films necessitated a different approach. They needed storylines with greater substance than the simple erecting of a radio aerial on a rooftop, or an attempt to start out on a picnic, or the delivery of a 'music box' up a long flight of steps. They would need subplots and straight actors and love stories and all manner of ploys that were not the stuff of which the world of Laurel and Hardy was made.

They entered into this new phase of their career with considerable enthusiasm. The knowledge that their audience felt about them the way it did was an undoubted factor in their approach. The British comedy duo Morecambe and Wise are perhaps the only pair who have drawn a similar response from audiences. From the moment they became aware that their popularity carried another, unexpected dimension their attitude changed too. As Ernie Wise observes: 'It gives you a great feeling, and it also makes you feel very responsible not to let [the audience] down.'

In time, through no fault of Laurel and Hardy's, audiences would feel let down, but for now the pair were embarked upon a new stage in their careers and cannot have been aware that they were inadvertently stepping on to a dangerous path. At first it was far from apparent, for they began well enough with some well-made films into which their comic style could blend without harm to either element.

Fra Diavolo (1933) is based upon Auber's comic opera and has the Boys (Stanlio and Ollio) as victims of bandits in eighteenth-century Italy. When their life savings are stolen they decide that the best way to recoup their loss is to become bandits themselves. One of the first people they hold-up is the notorious Fra Diavolo (the Devil's Brother), played by Dennis King. As if that were not bad enough, Ollio pretends to be Fra Diavolo.

Although understandably displeased at this the bandit chief decides to use the Boys in his plan to rob Lord and Lady Rocberg (Finlayson and Thelma Todd). In this way the Boys become reasonably well integrated into the main thrust of the film and their comic capers keep things moving along briskly enough. One engaging sequence has Stanlio helping Ollio pour wine from a cask into a large pitcher by means of a smaller vessel. Not bright enough to tell Ollio when the pitcher is full, Stanlio solves the problem by drinking every succeeding jug until he is well and truly drunk or, as Ollio puts it, 'spiffed'.

Fra Diavolo has a certain stately charm which helps to account for the manner in which the film stands up well today despite a certain datedness in its construction.

Having been out of their customary costume for their roles as eighteenth-century Italian robbers, the Boys stayed away from their derbies but changed to the other side of the law for *The Midnight Patrol* (1933), a two-reeler in which they were officers of law but very little order. In another two-reeler, *Busy Bodies* (1933), the team

Only fair cops in The Midnight Patrol.

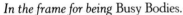

In the frame for being Busy Bodies.

wreaks predictable disorder at a building company, while in *Dirty Work* (1933) the Boys play chimney-sweeps, a prelude to disaster if ever there were one. As their customer is a mad scientist the outcome is even more catastrophic than if they had been let loose in an empty house.

Although dialogue still took second place to action, the Boys had discovered that certain lines could be used to good effect from movie to movie. Here, after Stan has inadvertently knocked Ollie off the roof and into a greenhouse, he asks him if he has been hurt. 'I have *nothing* to say,' Ollie replies with remarkable dignity. At the end of the movie, Ollie becomes the victim of the mad scientist's plan for rejuvenation when he is tumbled into a vat of chemicals. When he emerges he has regressed to a chimpanzee. The animal, complete with Ollie's derby and voice, makes the same declaration: 'I have *nothing* to say.'

There is also the excessively formal introduction by Ollie of himself and Stan: 'My name is Mr

Oliver Norvell Hardy and this is my friend Mr Laurel.' And, of course, there is his regular despairing comment (frequently misquoted): 'Here's another nice mess you've gotten me into.'

Their next feature film, *Sons of the Desert* (1933), struck an ideal balance between the expected sight gags, funny dialogue and the more complex plot demands of the longer format. The Boys are members of a fraternity whose socializing excludes wives. While this hardly pleases the Boys' respective spouses (Mae Busch as Mrs Hardy and Dorothy Christy as Mrs Laurel), the forthcoming convention in Chicago to which all members of the Boys' lodge are urged to go is guaranteed to cause marital friction.

Ollie, of course, maintains an air of lofty superiority as he asks Stan: 'Do you have to ask your wife everything?'

'Well,' replies Stan, 'if I didn't ask her, I wouldn't know what she wanted me to do.'

Stan and Ollie devise a scheme which will allow

With Charley Chase in Sons of the Desert.

With the murderous Mae Busch in Oliver the Eighth.

Another jacket Going Bye-Bye!

An unscheduled bath in Them Thar Hills.

them to take a boat trip for Ollie's health (Mrs Hardy is a bad sailor), but instead they head for Chicago. At the convention the Boys enjoy a high old time despite the practical jokes of Charley Chase. Unfortunately, the ship on which they are supposed to be cruising sinks and their wives are suitably disturbed. The ladies head for the shipping company's offices and in the meantime the Boys return home, see the newspaper headlines about the sinking, and panic.

Attempting to take their minds off the possible loss of their husbands, Mae and Dorothy visit a movie theatre and see a newsreel about the Chicago convention in which their supposedly sinking spouses are clearly visible. When the irate ladies return home the Boys hide in the attic but they make enough racket to alarm the girls, who go upstairs to investigate. After taking refuge on the roof the Boys are eventually confronted by their better halves. Stan admits all, which proves wise as Dorothy assures him that honesty is the best policy and takes him home for a delightful reunion. Ollie, however, still clinging on to his shredded lie, is attacked by Mae with a barrage of well-aimed pots and pans.

A string of shorts followed, including *Going Bye-Bye!* (1934), in which a criminal (Walter Long again) is understandably annoyed when the Boys' evidence sends him to jail (and positively enraged when Stan asks the judge, 'Aren't you going to hang him?') and is determined to wreak revenge; another in this sequence was *Them Thar Hills* (1934), in which the Boys and Mae Busch become exceedingly mellow thanks to the moonshine tipped in the well of an old shack in the mountains by the local bootleggers. Then Stan and Ollie returned to costume for another feature film which, like *Fra Diavolo*, originated on the musical stage.

Babes in Toyland (1934) is very much in the old tradition of the fairy story-cum-pantomime, although its immediate origins lay in a Victor Herbert musical comedy. Stannie Dum and Ollie Dee live in Toyland, where their talents, such as they are, have gained them fairly useful employment working for the toymaker, one of whose customers is Santa Claus. When Stannie confuses an order and makes 100 toy soldiers each six feet high instead of 600 soldiers one foot high they are fired. Also in trouble are Mother Peep and her beautiful daughter Bo (Florence Roberts and Charlotte Henry), whose evil landlord Silas Bar-

On the set for Babes in Toyland *with co-director Gus Meins, Henry Brandon, Florence Roberts and Charlotte Henry.*

naby (Henry Brandon) is eager to foreclose on their mortgage. The Boys determine to help, and during the ensuing complications Bo-Peep agrees to marry Barnaby even though she loves Tom-Tom (Felix Knight). Stannie is persuaded to stand in for Bo-Peep, a deception aided by a very thick veil.

Eventually Barnaby is pursued into Bogeyland, where he recruits the Bogeymen and returns to attack Toyland. The Boys do their best to defend their home and finally succeed thanks to the 100 six-foot soldiers, who rout the evil enemy.

Barnaby apart, everyone, as always happens in fairy tales, lives happily ever after.

A frequently screened favourite on American TV at Christmastime, *Babes in Toyland* is not as

thoroughly soft-centred as might well have been the case. Indeed, the baddies, especially the Bogeymen, are memorably unpleasant.

Back in derbies, seedy suits and two-reelers, the Boys were in cahoots (for once) with Walter Long in *The Live Ghost* (1934), in which they help him recruit some fairly able-bodied seamen for his ship. This activity ends with them shanghai'd too – a fate made worse by the ship's reputation of having a ghost aboard. When the drunken mate (Arthur Housman, one of Hollywood's finest drunk impersonators) falls in a tray of whitewash and commences to roam the vessel, chaos ensues.

In the well-titled *Tit For Tat* (1935), a sequel to *Them Thar Hills*, the Boys engage in reciprocal vengeance with fellow shopkeeper Charlie Hall,

Babes in Toyland *under another title.*

Our Gang's Spanky McFarland visits the set of Tit For Tat.

while in *The Fixer Uppers* and *Thicker Than Water* (both 1935) they tangle with, respectively, the jealous husband of a *femme fatale* (Mae Busch) and a suspiciously shrewish Mrs Hardy (Daphne Pollard).

In *The Fixer Uppers* they are Christmas-card salesmen, but with Stan responsible for the verses they are not doing too well. Among his poetic gems, delivered in Ollie's orotund tones, are:

'Twas Christmas Day in the poorhouse,
And the boys were feeling blue.
The boys in grey were fighting,
A merry Christmas to you.

and:

Jingle bells, jingle bells, coming through the rye,
I wish you a merry Christmas, even as you and I.

Another, especially for mothers, reads:

Merry Christmas, Mother, merry Christmas, Ma,
Hi, Mommy, Mommy and a hot-cha-cha.

The short films which had proved so successful for Laurel and Hardy in both the silent era and in the talkies were now jettisoned by the studio. From this point onwards the pair concentrated on feature films. The results were mixed – some excellent, some with good parts spread thinly through less than satisfactory material. What the Boys cannot have foreseen was that they were entering the final stages of their association with Hal Roach and, coincidentally, the last period in which they made movies that were generally acceptable to their audiences.

Pondering their next move in Bonnie Scotland.

CHAPTER SIX

Their First Mistake

End of an Era

'The longer it goes, the tougher it is to make a
good comedy.'

Hal Roach

Stan and daughter Lois on the lot in 1935.

The private lives of Stan and Babe had not been running as smoothly as their film careers. Stan's on-again, off-again life with Lois had been severely jolted by the death, in 1930, of their son, Stanley Robert, at only nine days old. The hard work into which Stan eventually threw himself probably helped him over a period of personal crisis, but it was a method which excluded his wife, whose distress was certainly no less than his. During the next few years their marriage went through a series of choppy patches. Between the rift and the eventual divorce Stan had affairs with other women, and then met Virginia Ruth Rogers. With her, he went through a marriage ceremony before his divorce was final. Therefore, when they were married in 1935, the press had scope to make much of his apparent view, a peculiarly Victorian one, that a woman compromised was a woman to be married.

His relationship with Ruth, however, proved fiery and was not helped by his drinking. None of his off-screen activities did much to endear him to Hal Roach, either, who worried over getting the required work out of Stan and the bad light he reflected on the studio. Roach's and Stan's attitude towards one another caused difficulties, too. Stan wanted Laurel and Hardy to be jointly contracted to the studio, while Roach, who believed that Stan could not look after his own affairs and needed the studio more than it needed him, did not.

Stan's lifestyle in the mid-1930s was such that he might well have become a very rich man had he not cluttered his personal life with the kinds of problem which led, inevitably in Hollywood, to high alimony payments. In the event, as his biographer Fred Guiles has pointed out, Stan continued to see Alyce Ardell, his long-time mistress, even after marrying Ruth and it is unsurprising, therefore, that this marriage fizzled out after a couple of years.

Babe's private life was also reaching a crisis point. He and Myrtle separated in 1935 and in 1937 they were divorced. Curiously enough, the press appeared uninterested, or perhaps was simply ill-informed about him; either way, he rarely made the gossip pages.

Set against their private lives, Stan's and Babe's movies were almost, but not quite, prosaic. In their feature *Bonnie Scotland* (1935) Stan inherits part of the estate of his grandfather Angus McLaurel. The bequest turns out to be only a snuffbox and a set of bagpipes while the bulk of the estate goes to another relative, Lorna (June Lang), who leaves to join her guardian in India. She is soon followed there by the Boys, who have accidentally joined the army. After various encounters with a grizzled sergeant (James Finlayson), Stan and Ollie inadvertently prevent a disaster when villainous natives set a trap for the regiment. Eventually, the Boys help reunite Lorna with her true love Alan (William Janney). Although this film has its moments it suffers from weak plotting and inadequate dialogue. Some of the sight gags are well devised but overall it proved to be a disappointment to the fans, who had hoped that Laurel and Hardy's permanent move into features would mean corresponding improvement upon the team's previously high standards.

Among the good scenes is one where Stan grills a fish by using a candle beneath the bedsprings, and there is also a well-performed version of the old gag about the only man in step in a parade. As the regiment marches along everyone is in step except Stan, who draws Ollie's attention to the fact that they are not together. Ollie changes step, tells the man next to him and gradually the entire regiment adjusts to Stan's step, until only the sergeant major at the head of the column is left. When his attention is drawn to the fact he gratefully acknowledges his error and changes step. As Peter Barnes commented in an article in *Films and Filming* in August 1960, this sequence is a good example of how Stan, 'the classic simpleton, the odd-man-out, far from being ostracized, finally converts the normal people to his way of thinking and seeing'. Had such a sequence appeared in a Chaplin film, Barnes suggests, it might well have been acclaimed by critics as a 'devastating satire on the herd instinct and the military machine', or in other such abstractions. The fact that this was a Laurel and Hardy film, and one of their lesser efforts to boot, meant that the critics ignored it – if indeed they bothered even to see it.

For *The Bohemian Girl* (1936) the Boys returned to the land of mittel-European operetta (the original is by Michael Balfe) but without displaying the flair of *Fra Diavolo*. Here again their comedy routines are slotted into an otherwise straight plot in such a manner that they are never fully integrated into the movie, but the comic sequences are mostly adequate without being truly inventive. One of the best, which shows Stan becoming steadily more inebriated while bottling wine, is a splendid example of his talent as a master of pantomime but does owe something to a similar sequence in *Fra Diavolo*. For the most part the rest of the cast fell a little short of the earlier film, despite appearances by the excellent Mae Busch, Thelma Todd and James Finlayson. The music was similarly a little below standard, although the score does include Balfe's best-known song, 'I Dreamt I Dwelt in Marble Halls'.

During production Thelma Todd was found dead in her car in the garage at her home. Her death was never fully explained. She appeared to have had no reason for suicide, but even if she had, there were means at her disposal other than asphyxiation. Out of respect, much of the footage she had already shot was excised from the movie.

It was at this time that relations between Stan and Hal Roach slumped. Aside from Roach's fears for bad publicity and Stan's eagerness to have Laurel and Hardy as a legal partnership under a single contract, Roach appeared to consider Laurel and Hardy to be his creation and he disliked, resented perhaps, any independence they might seek. Additionally Roach, ever far-sighted, was beginning to think in broader terms than continuing merely as a maker of comedy films. When Stan jibbed at re-signing his contract a deal was worked out which afforded him little financial benefit but much more control over their future productions. Consequently, the pair's next two features were billed as Stan Laurel Productions, giving them (or rather Stan) more real autonomy. It cannot have been coincidence that there was a marked improvement not only in the production values but also in the overall quality of the films.

Even without make-up Stan displays a perfect clown's face (The Bohemian Girl).

Keeping warm in The Bohemian Girl.

Bert and Alf in Our Relations.

In *Our Relations* (1936) Stan and Ollie are their customary landlocked selves complete with (fairly) amiable wives (Betty Healy and Daphne Pollard), but each has a ne'er-do-well twin brother, Alfie Laurel and Bert Hardy, who has not been seen for many years. Alf and Bert, who are sailors on the SS *Periwinkle*, are permanently broke, despite attempts by their shipmate Finn (James Finlayson) to make them save money. Persuaded by Finn to leave their pay with him, the sailor Boys go ashore with a package the captain (Sidney Toler) wants delivered to Denker's Beer Garden. At Denker's they share a glass of beer, all that they can afford; then, when Bert opens the package and discovers a valuable ring, they find themselves the centre of attention for a dubious waiter named Groagan (Alan Hale) and a couple of dockside floozies, Lily and Alice (Lona Andre and Iris Adrian). After accidentally wrecking the bar's telephone booth, the sailor Boys are compelled to leave the captain's ring as security while they try to raise the money. To do this they steal Finn's clothes and pawn them.

During all this, the landlocked Boys are meeting their wives outside, of all places, Denker's Beer Garden. Once inside Stan and Ollie cannot understand the behaviour of Groagan and are mortified when Lily and Alice appear and criticize their latest choice in feminine company. Needless to say, Betty and Daphne are not well pleased with any of this. When the Boys pay their bill the ring is handed to them and their wives react

predictably, refusing to believe any protestations that the ring is a mystery to their husbands. The arrival of Finn, complete with pictures of Alf and Bert in the company of some babes in bathing-suits, serves only to fuel the wives' fury.

When Alf and Bert return to Denker's in an attempt to recover the ring, the naturally irate Groagan throws them out and in the ensuing *mêlée* the sailor Boys are arrested and carried off to jail. On the way they are spotted by a friend of the wives, who alerts Betty and Daphne. They promptly go down to the court and help the suitably surprised sailor Boys gain their release. The wives take Alf and Bert for a celebratory drink at the Pirate Club – which is where Stan and Ollie have decided to have their own celebration. The arrival of Lily and Alice serves only to precipitate another round of mistaken identities. When the ship's captain turns up demanding his ring back from the wrong pair further complications ensue. Among these are the momentary and mutually confusing teaming of Alf with Ollie and a chase through the pirate-ship rigging which decorates the nightclub.

Kidnapped by crooks with eyes on the captain's valuables, Stan and Ollie are given a cement footbath and threatened with instant immersion in the harbour. The arrival of look-alikes Alf and

Bert spreads confusion and fear through the crooks, the cops and one another. Finally the Boys and the sailor Boys realize who is who and what has been happening. Arm in arm they stroll off only for Ollie and Bert to fall into the dock – which does not surprise Stan and Alf one little bit.

A most enjoyable film, *Our Relations* benefits from high production values and good photography by Rudolph Maté, who later turned to directing and had many action films to his credit.

Among the qualities which raised this film above other features the Boys made was the simple yet often overlooked fact that the entire story is about Laurel and Hardy. They are the meat of the film – not merely characters who provide comic relief. Of course there is not the sustained sight-gag inventiveness of the two-reelers, but that results not from lack of ideas but from a better understanding of the role that the pair needed to occupy in the longer format.

The fact that this film and their next, *Way Out West* (1937), which was even more successful, were produced under Stan Laurel's control lends considerable weight to the argument that he was the major force in the development of the team.

As *Way Out West* begins Stan and Ollie come to the little cow-town of Brushwood Gulch, where they plan to deliver the title deeds of a goldmine to Mary Roberts (Rosina Lawrence), the daughter of a recently deceased friend of theirs. The owner and bartender of the local saloon, Mickey Finn (James Finlayson), knows a good thing when he spots one and hastily tells the Boys that he will introduce them to Mary. Instead, he sends his wife Lola (Sharon Lynne) to the Boys, having first briefed her on the part she is to play. Pretending to be Mary, she succeeds in obtaining the deeds, but soon afterwards the Boys meet the real Mary, who is the saloon's maid-of-all-work.

Failing to recover the deeds, thanks largely to the intervention of the sheriff, with whom they have already tangled, the Boys leave town. Determined to help Mary, they sneak back at night, break into the saloon and, after some destructive sparring with Finn, grab the deeds and Mary and make their escape.

The sight gags in *Way Out West* are well thought out and while there may be nothing especially original about them they do have the timelessness that comes in part from the fact that the Boys were never weary of, nor afraid to use, old jokes. Instead, they regarded them, as did their fans, as old and well-loved possessions to be taken out on occasion and lovingly repolished.

The predictability with which Ollie steps into the impossibly deep pothole each time they cross the stream just outside Brushwood Gulch is one example; the byplay with the rope with which Stan hopefully hauls Ollie up to an upper-storey window is another. Stan's decision to let go of the rope to spit on his hands is just plain commonsense; the fact that he chooses to do this while Ollie is suspended in mid-air is sheer hard luck. Then there is a marvellously contagious scene when Stan's ticklishness reduces him to hysteria as he is searched by Lola.

Among the many highlights of the film is the music. One featured song, by Marvin Hatley, is 'Won't You Be My Lovey Dovey?' while the best-remembered occurs in the scene in which Stan and Ollie join in a song being sung in the saloon. Ollie's gentle tenor and Stan's harmonizing make a delightful musical interlude, until the comedy returns as Stan's voice switches from deepest bass (provided by Chill Wills) to soprano (Rosina Lawrence), after Ollie has tapped his head with a mallet. Forty years later, and much to the surprise of almost everyone, 'The Trail of the Lonesome Pine' was released as a single and became a hit in the British pop charts.

Heading for trouble (Way Out West).

The Boys and Rosina Lawrence are ordered out by James Finlayson in Way Out West.

The mule's the one in the middle (Way Out West).

*Room for one more inside (*Way Out West*).*

Thinly disguised as Mexicans for Pick a Star.

With the two Stan Laurel productions completed, the Boys returned to the format of the operetta into which their comedy routines were inserted without too much concern for integration. Having failed in America as itinerant mousetrap salesmen, the Boys, in *Swiss Miss* (1938), seek their fortunes in Switzerland. Far from improving, their business is so bad that they have not sold a single mousetrap in the two weeks they have been in the country. Without a bean between them, they are obliged to wash dishes at an hotel when they cannot pay for their meal. They learn that one of the hotel's guests is the famous composer Victor Albert (Walter Woolf

King). He is having a hard time with his new opera partly due to his love for Anna (Della Lind), for whom Ollie also develops a momentary passion, unaware that she and Victor are already married.

Among the complications in which the Boys find themselves is one brilliantly devised and sustained gag based on the task of carrying Victor's piano up to a tree-house high in the mountains. Along the way they have to cross a swaying rope-bridge, a task made doubly difficult by the appearance of a gorilla. The gorilla-on-the-bridge gag is a good one, although it suffers from inexplicable editing by the studio, which completely omitted to show a bomb, designed to go off when a certain key is struck, being rigged up in the piano. The frequent occasions on which Stan accidentally crashes on to the piano's keyboard are therefore rendered meaningless.

One gag which did remain untouched shows Stan, amply demonstrating his talent for mime, persuading a St Bernard dog that he (Stan) is a freezing mountaineer trapped in a snowstorm (so that the dog, thoroughly confused, gives up his cask of brandy) when in fact he is merely sitting outside the hotel kitchen plucking chickens in a cloud of drifting feathers.

Some scenes for *Swiss Miss* were shot in colour (Della Lind suggests that an entire colour version was made), but the only known prints are in black and white.

The off-screen discord at Hal Roach Productions had not passed unnoticed and when the Boys made *Block-Heads* (1938) it was widely rumoured that this would be the last Laurel and Hardy movie. The disagreements still rested upon Stan's belief that he should be allowed to create the gags for their films unencumbered by less deft hands. It is a matter for unprofitable debate just how much Roach's incursion into what Stan regarded as his territory was merely that of a concerned producer for work being done under his aegis (and for which he was paying substantial sums of money) and how much was genuine interference. In the event the new film turned out not to be their last, nor indeed was it their last for Roach. But it was the last under the old system of production. As it turned out, it was also very nearly the last film of any stature they were to make.

Block-Heads begins with the Boys in the trenches during World War I. Left behind to guard the post when Ollie and the rest of the platoon leave the trench to attack the enemy, Stan begins his march up and down.

Time passes – twenty years in fact – and Stan is still marching up and down in a trench, this one worn by two decades of his pacing. He breaks off for a meal from a can of beans, and when he tosses the empty can away it increases the mountain of empty cans that overshadows the post. Finally discovered, he returns to America, where Ollie is celebrating the first anniversary of his wedding. After a slight contretemps with the lady in the adjoining apartment, Mrs Gilbert (Patricia Ellis), and her husband (played by Billy Gilbert), who is newly returned from big-game hunting in Africa, Ollie heads out to buy his wife a gift with the dollar he has had to borrow from her. On the way he sees the newspaper reports about his former comrade-in-arms and immediately heads for the old soldiers' home.

Stan is happy and comfortable at the home, although the chair he happens to be using in the grounds could be better. He accommodates the fact that he is occupying a chair designed for a one-legged man by sitting with one of his legs doubled up beneath him. When Ollie arrives it appears to him that his old pal has only one leg.

Ollie invites Stan to his apartment, assuring him that Mrs Hardy will be delighted to meet, feed and board him. After carrying Stan to his car Ollie discovers that he is not a cripple and irritably orders him to move the truck that is blocking the car. Stan, being somewhat behind the times where machinery is concerned, pulls the wrong lever and the truck's load of sand tips on to the car in which Ollie is already sitting.

Back at the apartment building where Ollie lives Stan's introduction to the marvels of modern technology continues when Ollie explains how the garage doors open automatically when the car is driven over a special plate. Stan asks if he can have a go. Needless to say, he misses the plate and wrecks both car and garage.

Before they reach the apartment (thirteen floors up and the lift out of order) Ollie has been in a scrap with a neighbour (James Finlayson), learnt that an ex-girlfriend, unaware that he is now a happily married man, has left a note for him inside, and has had a set-to with a small boy, his football and his father.

In the apartment Stan takes a glass of water from his pocket, drinks, then at Ollie's sarcastic

Carrying the piano and . . .

. . . the tuba in Swiss Miss

109

Old pals . . .

. . . but not for long (in Block-Heads*).*

suggestion adds ice-cubes he pulls from another pocket. If that was a touch of Harpo Marx, Stan's next move makes another of his occasional excursions into 'white' magic. Using his hand as a pipe, he stuffs the palm with tobacco, lights it, sucks on his thumb and blows smoke at the astonished Ollie.

The arrival of Mrs Hardy (Minna Gombell) does nothing to enhance the spirit of reunion between the old comrades. She takes an instant dislike to Stan and promptly goes home to her mother. The Boys decide to make a meal, which results in the wrecking of the kitchen in a gas explosion. Mrs Gilbert (Patricia Ellis's character) comes from across the hall to help but is drenched in the contents of a punchbowl; discovering she is locked out, she changes into a pair of Ollie's pyjamas: cue for the return of Mrs Hardy. The Boys fling a cover over Mrs Gilbert, who pretends to be an armchair. Eventually, they transfer her to a trunk, which is where she stays until her husband appears. Stan confides in him that a girl is hidden in the trunk. Mr Gilbert boasts that this is not the way to handle affairs and that he has girls all over the place. (This sequence draws susbtantially from the central plot of *Unaccustomed As We Are*.) When Mrs Gilbert rises furiously from the trunk the big-game hunter runs to fetch his elephant gun and chases the Boys out of the apartment. When he looses off a few shots half-dressed men leap from every window.

The closing gag was, of course, a straight lift from *We Faw Down* and was added by the studio when Stan was absent (he had wanted to show his and Ollie's heads mounted on the wall like trophies). Despite the lack of originality in material, it is all carried off with considerable panache and today's audiences find it hard to understand the lack of enthusiasm with which *Block-Heads* was greeted by critics of the time, except for the fact that they tended to give the thumbs-down to any Laurel and Hardy movie.

During 1938, the pair made one of their occasional stabs at radio but failed to find a sponsor. The pilot show, *The Wedding Party*, was subsequently issued as a gramophone record.

Rumours of an end to the partnership of Laurel and Hardy were given impetus by the appearance of Ollie in a movie with Harry Langdon. A film about two amiable incompetents and a pet elephant would have seemed to be a likely vehicle for the Boys, but in the event it was Ollie and the once massively popular Langdon who made it. *Zenobia* (1939) might well have appeared to be an attempt by Roach to spark a new partnership, but it was probably just convenient all round. Laurel and Hardy had never been contracted as a team and their individual contracts were out of step. When Laurel's lapsed, he decided this time to wait until his partner's came up for renewal so that they could renegotiate jointly. Stan had also been talking to Mack Sennett, who had not given up hope that he might once more enter the comedy-film stakes. For Hardy, the role of Henry Tebbitt in *Zenobia* was an opportunity to play an almost straight comic part, something which he had clearly loved doing in his earlier years. For Harry Langdon, the film was a chance to hit the comeback trail – albeit one that did not work out.

Looking into the future with palmist Guy Kelsey.

Langdon and Hardy, a temporary partnership (Zenobia).

For Roach, it meant that the time while Hardy was under contract but not working with Laurel would not be entirely wasted and the projected movie could go ahead regardless.

In the event, the hiatus soured relationships between Hal Roach and Stan Laurel and a lawsuit compounded the disaffection. Stan was charged with being unco-operative and having violated the morals clause in his contract (a standard clause in Hollywood contracts of the time). As Fred Guiles has pointed out, such a charge deeply affected Stan, who was, if anything, too moral. Had he not believed so sincerely in marriage but been prepared to have an occasional fling, he might well

The Boys with Hal Roach.

have ended his days a much richer, though not necessarily a happier, man. He might also have avoided the sensational headlines which dogged him and irritated Roach.

Stan's marriage to Ruth burned out and in January 1938 he married a Russian-born singer and dancer known professionally as Illeana. A month earlier, during the closing stages of his divorce from Ruth, the press had titillated its readers with reports of the return from Australia of Mae Dahlberg to make financial demands on Stan.

The marriage to Illeana was also a short-lived affair and the fact that the conflict with Roach arose at the time when he was once more heading for the divorce courts did nothing to help Stan through a particularly trying time. Nevertheless, he was determined to fight the court case and, more importantly, to bring his, and Babe's, career under his control. He wanted desperately, though

belatedly, to gain the same measure of control over their work that Chaplin had had over his. Additionally, and with considerable justification, he sought the financial reward his many years of dedication to the art of film comedy had surely earned him. Unfortunately he had left it too late, and had also drastically misjudged the state of the film world and the attitudes and responses of the film audience.

Resolutions of sorts were, however, in the air. As Stan's marriage to Illeana began its collapse and before their divorce in 1940, he began seeing Ruth again. They were to re-marry in 1941.

By now Babe Hardy was free of Myrtle, but instead of marrying his long-time mistress Viola Morse, he allowed his head to be turned by a pretty continuity girl working on the new movie the Boys signed to make together towards the end of 1939. It was two years before Babe married Lucille Jones, but on this occasion it was to prove third time lucky for him.

The new film, for which the Boys went to RKO, was *The Flying Deuces* (1939). The story opens in Paris, where Ollie is enamoured of Georgette (Jean Parker), whom he plans to marry. Georgette turns him down. Hurt beyond redress, Ollie decides to end it all in the river Seine, where he thinks Stan should join him.

When his reluctant pal demurs, Ollie upbraids him: 'So that's the kind of guy you are. After all I've done for you! Do you realize that after I'm gone you'll just go on living by yourself? People would stare at you and wonder what you are. And I wouldn't be there to tell them. There'd be no one to protect you. Do you want that to happen to you?'

Tearfully, Stan admits: 'I never thought of that. I'm sorry if I hurt your feelings, Ollie. I didn't mean to be so impolite.'

A believer in reincarnation, Ollie thinks he will come back as a horse, but before he can put his beliefs to the test François (Reginald Gardiner) comes by. He is an officer of the French Foreign Legion and he convinces them that the Legion is the best way to forget the past. The Boys agree and hasten to join, diverted only momentarily when Stan tosses the rock that is tied to Ollie into the Seine.

Once in uniform the Boys quickly realize that this is not the life for them. Faced with one mountain of laundry and another of vegetables needing peeling, Ollie decides that the experience

On camera in 1938.

A delicate touch to the laundry (Flying Deuces).

has worked. He came here to forget and he has forgotten, so now he can go home. The Legion does not see it in quite this light, however. The Boys head for the airport, where the arrival of Georgette does not help matters, especially when it turns out that she has come to join her husband, François. Classed as deserters, the Boys are put in the guardhouse, where they are in the care of a jailer played by James Finlayson. Their incarceration is only temporary as they are to be shot at sunrise. This fact is driven home to a discomfited Ollie when Stan, using his bedsprings as a harp, plaintively plucks out 'The World is Waiting for the Sunrise'.

Escaping from their cell by way of an existing tunnel, the Boys frighten Georgette (inexplicably the tunnel terminates in her room) before heading for the airfield and hiding in an aircraft which accidentally takes off. When the plane crashes Ollie goes off to heaven while Stan survives only to meet a horse that speaks to him in Ollie's voice. Remembering his pal's wishes about reincarnation, Stan is not at all surprised. 'Gee, I'm glad to see you,' he tells him.

Ollie edges Stan out of Jean Parker's affections in Flying Deuces.

Although there were a number of old Roach hands involved in the making of *The Flying Deuces*, the film was a long way from being an effective vehicle for the Boys. Most times the re-working of old material resulted in a new twist here and there, or at least a fine-tuning of some routine, a polishing of a little bit of business. The difference here is that there is no apparent improvement on the old material. Indeed, there are clear signs of tiredness, which is perhaps to be expected since now, in 1939, the Boys were pushing 50 and had worked almost non-stop as a team for a dozen years, during which time they had made about 90 films.

After the film was released Hal Roach, with whom Stan had eventually contracted to make four movies, offered a deal. Stan was in need of money to help straighten out his tangled personal affairs and if he hesitated at the thought of working again with Roach it was not for long.

In the event it was a changed Roach who worked with Stan on preparations for the new film. Hal Roach's son, Hal Roach Jr, was an associate producer on the Roach lot, which was by now headlining a very different kind of film to those of their heyday as leaders in the field of broad comedy. Comedy was still a significant factor of the studio's production schedule, but it was now the sophisticated kind demonstrated in *Topper* (1937, starring Cary Grant, Constance Bennett and Roland Young) and its successors. There were also straight dramas such as the masterly film version of John Steinbeck's *Of Mice and Men* (1940), and such fantasies as *One Million B.C.* (1940), which starred Carole Landis. (In 1966 Hal Roach co-produced the British re-make *One Million Years B.C.*, featuring Raquel Welch.) Despite Roach's deep involvement with other matters he was happy to let his son relieve the pressure so that he could personally handle

A rueful undergraduate in A Chump at Oxford.

production of the new Laurel and Hardy film.

Many of the gags used in *A Chump at Oxford* (1940) are old material, but this time there is no sign of staleness. Stan and Roach had obviously buried their differences at least deep enough to allow their collaboration to be creative and lively.

Tenuously employed as street cleaners, the Boys break for lunch. A banana peel tossed away by Stan brings about the downfall of a bank robber. The bank president is so grateful he offers the Boys anything they want. They know what is holding them back: lack of education. The president is as good as his word and soon the Boys are on their way to Oxford. After surviving a ragging by a group of other students (including 26-year-old Peter Cushing, many years away from his Hammer horror career) and a run-in with the Dean (Wilfred Lucas), the Boys meet their valet Meredith (Forrester Harvey), who immediately recognizes Stan. Meredith is sure that Stan is really Lord Paddington, the scholastic and athletic genius who disappeared after losing his memory many years ago. Ollie does not believe this for a moment and Stan is quick to agree that he is too dumb. When the students arrive outside their room ready for more trouble Stan looks out and the window drops on his head, which is exactly how Lord Paddington lost his memory. Instantly, the process is reversed. Lord Paddington is back and celebrates by first beating up the gang of students (and in the process heaving the Dean and Ollie out of the window). Despite Lord Paddington's mental superiority he keeps Ollie on as his manservant, explaining in upper-crust accents that Fattie, as he calls him, has 'a jolly old face, you know . . . and helps fill up the room.' When the irritated Ollie finally snaps and declares he is leaving Oxford to return to America, Lord Paddington is unconcerned, but then the students arrive to sing 'For He's a Jolly Good Fellow' outside the window. Stan looks out, the window crashes down, and Ollie's old pal is once more as dumb as ever.

A Chump at Oxford was a marked improvement over their most recent efforts and remains popular to this day. Not least among its qualities is Stan's performance which, given the storyline, is necessarily much more deeply textured than usual. At the time of its release, Laurel and Hardy fans were pleased at this sign that the team was in good shape and capable of resisting competition (Abbott and Costello were then on the brink of their takeover as the screen's most financially successful comedy duo).

Unfortunately, the success of Chump was not the harbinger of a resurgence in the careers of Laurel and Hardy. Part of the problem was that they were still making movies which while technically classed as features were too short to warrant top billing. Although anything that raised a smile on the world's face in 1940 was something of great value, the Boys were being overtaken by one of show business's great imponderables. The passage of the next few decades would prove that their comedy was timeless but they were temporarily stuck in a period when public tastes in entertainment were undergoing change.

For the moment, however, the fact that they were on the brink of the final downhill phase of their career was not apparent. Early in 1940, the Boys began work on the second film that Stan owed to Hal Roach under his contract. It was to be their last with Roach and while far from being their best it was, at least, one which their fans can view without discomfort.

In Saps at Sea (1940) Stan and Ollie are working in a horn-making factory where the racket does little for Ollie's jangled nerves. Stan

Musical mis-mates tuning up for Saps at Sea.

takes his pal in search of medical assistance, a journey which proves almost as calamitous to Ollie's condition as the noisy factory. The jamming of the car horn is the least of his worries when they discover that the car's engine will only work when placed in the back seat. Eventually, Ollie is attended by 'Dr' Finlayson, who diagnoses 'hornophobia' (this was Fin's last appearance with the Boys after more than 30 films), and advises a sea voyage. Returning home to their apartment, the Boys are faced with more chaos, most of which is due to the activities of a maintenance

Games people play.

man (Ben Turpin) whose crossed eyes have resulted in such innovations as a fridge that plays music and an iced-up radio. While Ollie is downstairs remonstrating with Ben's character his pal begins a music lesson, but the sound of a trombone is too much for the returning Ollie, who goes wild.

Moments later, when Stan emerges from a cupboard in which he has been hiding, Ollie is flipped out of the window, where he hangs from the telephone wire. Going downstairs with a mattress, Stan lays it over his car and attempts to drive beneath the dangling Ollie. Instead he succeeds in demolishing the apartment house, much to the despair of the desk clerk (played by Charlie Hall in the last of *his* many roles with the team). By this time Ollie has fallen to the ground, just in time for Stan, who is backing his car out of the wrecked building, to run over him.

The fast-moving and lively re-working of many old comedy routines makes the first section of *Saps at Sea* a pleasure to watch. The rest of the film is much less good. On board the boat they have hired and which they intend keeping moored securely to the dockside, the Boys are joined by Nick (Rychard Cramer), a criminal on the run from the law. As unwilling hosts to the tough guy and equally unhappy at being at sea, the Boys are ordered to make a meal for Nick. With no food on board they set to with great gusto, concocting a feast out of string, soap, lamp-wick, talcum pow-

der and tobacco. They are not careful enough, however, and Nick, noticing their antics, forces them to eat the resulting mess. In desperation Stan plays his trombone, sending Ollie berserk and capable of tackling the gangster. The repeated collapse of the instrument is an impediment, for Ollie keeps lapsing into corresponding normality, but eventually they overcome the villain and return to the harbour, where the police are waiting. Unfortunately Stan blows his trombone again, Ollie thumps the harbour cop and the Boys are hauled off to prison – where they are to share a cell with Big Nick.

The films that followed, which were produced for Twentieth Century-Fox and MGM, proved to be flops which forever left a sour taste in the mouths of both the Boys and their fans. What is especially sad, given the poor quality of these remaining films, is that there is no evidence to suggest that their creativity was exhausted. They were eager to make more films, and in 1940 formed a joint production company: Laurel and Hardy Feature Productions. Stan was busily thinking up new ideas and concepts, and their private lives were settled (although in Stan's case this turned out to be a temporary situation).

Until this moment, however their success had been phenomenal. They had been working as a team for thirteen years and were the only film comics of their era to straddle the great divide between silents and talkies with total, if uneven, success.

If there were no comic duos who ranked with Laurel and Hardy there were many singles who could rightly be termed their peers if not their superiors. Yet none of these other great silent-film talents succeeded in making so successful a shift into talkies.

Was it that Laurel and Hardy had something extra or was it simply a failing of these others, notably Chaplin, Keaton and Lloyd, to adapt their undoubted genius to new demands?

Charlie Chaplin, a sometimes cruel genius.

CHAPTER SEVEN

Our Relations

Chaplin, Keaton and Lloyd

'Chaplin was the greatest.'

Stan Laurel

'Stan was the greatest; Charlie was second.'

Buster Keaton

Soon after entering the movies, Charlie Chaplin shot to heights of popularity that truly befitted a genius of film comedy. Unfortunately, in addition to general public popularity, Chaplin also met with the acclaim of the intelligentsia. This brought with it certain problems which were not apparent at the time but which subsequently affected his view of himself and his work. He changed, became less sympathetic and this, together with his inability to adapt and hence maintain his success after the arrival of talkies, prevented him from retaining his pre-eminent position in the consciousness of that same public which had earlier idolized him.

Chaplin's background bears some similarities to Stan Laurel's, although he was from a much poorer home – but perhaps not quite so poor as his sometimes self-serving autobiography suggests. His father, Charles Chaplin, was a music-hall artist as was his mother, Hannah Hill, who used the stage name Lily Harley. For all practical purposes young Charlie never knew life outside the theatre. Born in 1889, Charlie made his first stage appearance in Aldershot in 1894 and in 1898 he was a member of a clog-dancing troupe known as the Eight Lancashire Lads.

By 1901, the year in which his father died and his mother was first admitted to a hospital for the mentally sick, Charlie was a highly experienced trouper, still not in his teens. A few years later, as the leading light of Fred Karno's army of comic clowns with successes in Britain and Europe to his credit, he was ready to conquer the new world of motion pictures.

He had made two forays to America with

Karno troupes, one in 1910, the second in 1912, and had begun to approach a level of popularity there akin to that he enjoyed in his homeland. In Los Angeles he met up with Mack Sennett, who hired him to work with his Keystone company. It was an attraction of opposites – or it would have been if there had been much attraction. In fact Sennett was not too sure whether the small, quiet but cocky Englishman would be able to reproduce enough of his stage comedy to make the transition into films; as for Chaplin, he was uneasy at the loud, outrageously enthusiastic bunch of seemingly undisciplined gag-makers who inhabited the crazily comic world of Mack Sennett.

The team Chaplin joined included such diverse talents as Edgar Kennedy, Slim Summerville, Chester Conklin, Ford Sterling and Mabel Normand. Despite the talent all around him, Charlie's first film efforts did not work out very well and for a while it looked as if Sennett's early fears were right.

Chaplin's first three films were released close together in 1914. In *Making a Living* he is disappointing and quite unrecognizable to latter-day audiences in his smart clothes and large moustache. *Kid Auto Races at Venice* saw the introduction of his 'tramp' guise, though it was not to be a consistent part of his comic make-up at Keystone. The third film was *Mabel's Strange Predicament*. However shaky the start might have been a parade of successes was soon to materialize. Between December 1913 and November the following year, when an offer of $1,250 a week attracted him to Essanay, he turned out films in which his grasp of the techniques of film-making can be seen to be growing. He also convinced himself, and eventually Sennett too, that he should have complete control over his work. He got it, and clung to it for the rest of his working life, in sharp contrast to Stan Laurel.

At Essanay he began a series of films which made him a bigger star than anyone, even Charlie himself (who was never short on self-esteem), can have imagined. Partly contributing to his massive success was the fact that at Essanay he did not have to work to the established, frenetic Keystone style; additionally he had more time in which to work, as here there was no demand to turn out films in under a week; and above all, he was given an unqualified free hand. His inventiveness knew no bounds and neither, it seems, did his time- and money-consuming working methods. Recently unearthed film of Chaplin outtakes and rehearsal footage shows that the easy simplicity of many of his gags was the product of many hours of painstaking and meticulous construction.

Throughout all these early Chaplin films runs a current of often extreme violence. The use of violence for comic effect was, of course, a staple of silent films, but much of Chaplin's shows often quite startling levels of cruelty. Sometimes Charlie is on the receiving end but most often he is the perpetrator of kicks, jabs, punches, stabbings and general mayhem against men, women and children, many of whom were used merely as inanimate props.

In striking contrast there is also the pathos on which many, but by no means all, screen comics depended for injecting humanity into their comedies. In Chaplin's case pathos would in time change to bathos, with the inevitable weakening of his effect upon more sophisticated audiences. Long before that, however, Chaplin had built up a staggering catalogue of comic successes. And with his success came a worldwide following that has probably never been equalled, even though it was to prove less enduring than anyone in or out of Hollywood can have imagined in those early years.

It may seem unfair to lay the blame for Charlie's Little Fellow being overtaken by delusions of grandeur at the doors of the more intellectual critics, but there is some justification. Whatever the art form, there is never any shortage of people claiming to have observed qualities in a painting, book, play or movie which the creator never put there. 'Don't trust what the writer says, trust what he writes,' they urge, even though this frequently reduces the creative artist to little more than a pawn in the hands of some unknown, unexplained yet omniscient being. Such pretentious nonsense often serves to keep in work critics and educationalists who might, if the subjects of their wisdom were to return to vociferous life, suffer a rude awakening.

Charlie Chaplin did not make his early films for the intellectual stimulus of as-yet-unborn generations of movie critics. He made them primarily because he was driven (as are so many entertainers) by an ego which demanded that he should succeed. There was also the money, which, given Chaplin's origins, must have been a spur.

Once he became aware of the opinion of the critical intelligentsia Charlie's work underwent a change. He believed what they said of him, that his every gesture had meaning; as a result his every gesture became increasingly more meaningful. Fortunately, Chaplin's genius was sufficient to overcome the pretentiousness that now intruded in much of his work and which gave the critics even more to feed upon.

Had Chaplin heeded to the mass of filmgoers rather than the intellectual few, he might have managed to retain the early bond that existed between himself and his audience, just as Laurel and Hardy did with their audience (which was drawn from substantially the same strata of society). Instead, his overt concern that he should observe the clown's philosophical role in society detached him from the ordinary person his Little Fellow claimed to be. Also, astonishingly for a man of such perception in many respects, he failed to develop the character in the way in which Laurel and Hardy developed theirs. This failure to adapt, to move with the times, contributed eventually to the feeling of present-day audiences that the Little Fellow will not continue to exist after that last, often coy or unnecessarily sentimental fade-out. The Little Fellow was funny and sad, he made people laugh and cry, but he failed to live on in the hearts of his former audience.

Roy Castle, the British entertainer whose act at one time included an effective Stan Laurel impression, rightly considers Chaplin's comedy to be calculated, unlike that of Laurel and Hardy which appears to be more freely inspired. Such calculation may have contributed to the shift in audience response. Any comedian who seeks to raise laughs is manipulating his audience. In Chaplin's case, his approach to his work, matching as it did his careful control of the business side of his film career, makes the manipulation too obvious for comfort.

Chaplin's failure to come to terms with sound was a different matter. It would be absurd to imagine that he could not have achieved the transition earlier and at least as successfully as Stan Laurel. Although he was a Londoner by birth, Charlie's accent was no less acceptable than was Stan's. Neither can he have been incapable of developing comic dialogue (although when he did eventually make talkies the dialogue was never as effective as that devised for Laurel and Hardy). More probable reasons lay in the continued critical and popular success of his silent films, which continued even into the era of talking pictures, and the complications within Charlie's personal life, which stretched over the years of Hollywood's change-over to talkies.

Just as Stan Laurel's professional life was affected by his personal problems, so too was Charlie's. While making *The Gold Rush* (1925) Charlie had married his co-star Lita Grey, then 16 and already pregnant, which gave the press much to snap and snarl over. Lita had to be dropped from the film and soon from Charlie's life, although not before they had had two children. The resulting divorce proceedings were liberally scattered with accusations of sexual misbehaviour, and although this came some years after the case in which comedian Fatty Arbuckle was accused of causing the death of a young woman through sexual excesses and the case in which actresses Mabel Normand and Mary Miles Minter were allegedly involved in the murder of director William Desmond Taylor, the press had a field day.

Throughout the period of the divorce proceedings, which began early in 1927, Charlie was trying to make *The Circus* (1928) and simultaneously fend off the US Treasury, which was claiming more than $1 million in unpaid taxes. The puritan streak which lies alarmingly close to the surface of American life led to calls for his films to be banned and he suffered a nervous and emotional collapse. Chaplin's autobiography excludes this entire episode, marriage and all (the book's omissions are at least as revealing as its contents, however: Stan Laurel is another instance already noted).

Despite problems during its making *The Circus* won for Chaplin a special Oscar 'for versatility and genius in writing, acting, directing and producing'. Certainly by the time Charlie began work on *City Lights* (1931) he had recovered his equilibrium, but he appeared not to have taken any notice of the technical developments which had been taking place. True, he uses music (which he wrote), but no dialogue. Curiously enough, the absence of sound in the new all-talking, all-singing era was accepted and *City Lights* became one of the most popular and successful of his long films. Perhaps the opinion of one contemporary writer, that *City Lights* was an indictment of the current crop of talkies, reflects the poor quality of some early sound films. Such comments and the good business the movie did help explain Chaplin's seemingly mystifying decision to make another silent film as late as 1936. By this time silent film was an anachronism and however effective *Modern Times* might look when seen today as part of a Chaplin season, at the time it must have bewildered audiences – especially younger people for whom the silent movie was rapidly becoming a thing of the past.

When, in 1940, Chaplin released his first talkie, *The Great Dictator*, he had allowed a gap to grow between himself and many other, mostly lesser, comedy film-makers. This gap might not have been insurmountable for a young Chaplin but he was by then 51 years old and the impetus, if not the enthusiasm, necessary for making movies in an increasingly competitive and expensive world had gone. Charlie Chaplin was not finished yet, but his place in film history today would be barely affected had he not made anything after *Modern Times*.

Just as Chaplin's early years bore resemblances to Stan Laurel's, so too did the beginnings of another great silent clown, Buster Keaton.

Keaton was born into a show-business family in 1895. His father was a noted entertainer who worked medicine shows and vaudeville. The family's ethnic origins were somewhat hazy and remained so, especially after Buster began his rise to fame. Those origins may have been Irish or they could have been American Indian – some difference! Buster, named Joseph Francis, literally crawled on to the stage when he was nine months old; his intention was to discover what his father was doing. The appearance of a tiny, solemn-faced baby brought a laugh and Joe Sr, knowing a good thing when it was thrust upon him, thereafter retained his son in the act. That soon involved the child in a continuous series of rough-house routines wherein he was flung around the stage like a rag doll, thus learning, the hard way, how to take falls. The boy was an acrobat before he knew the meaning of the word and certainly before he could spell it, for education (the formal kind) was not something the Keaton troupe had time for.

Buster was given his name very early in life, allegedly by Harry Houdini, who worked the shows with the Keatons, although this may be another doubtful incident in the Keaton myth. On one point there was no doubt: Buster Keaton was soon recognized as a major talent and the fame of the Keatons (who included mother Myra, dubiously billed as America's first female saxophone player, and in time siblings Harry and Louise) spread throughout America. By the time he was in his early teens, Buster was the mainstay of the act and his stone-faced persona established. Audiences laughed very readily at this slightly-built kid whose own expression never cracked. Joe Sr spotted that too and insisted it stayed in the act.

Film-making was not in Joe's master plan; like many other vaudevilleans, he objected to the thought that audiences in movie theatres could see the great Keatons for a few cents when he knew they were worth big bucks. The 'flickers' were considered a come-down. When Buster ran across fellow vaudevillean-turned-movie-comic Roscoe 'Fatty' Arbuckle in New York in 1917 he had never thought of or been considered for a career in pictures.

Arbuckle had just left the Mack Sennett organization to sign with Russian-born promoter Joseph M. Schenck, who, accepting that he knew nothing about the movies except that he could make money out of producing them, left Arbuckle to his own devices. Arbuckle suggested Buster should join him in a film they were shooting; Buster did so, made a successful début and simultaneously met Schenck, who was to be a major influence in his career, and Schenck's sister-in-law, Natalie Talmadge, who was to become Buster's wife.

As Buster made more and more movies (the company soon moved to California) he learned fast, and very soon discovered how much he could achieve by inventive use of the camera. More than

any of the other great silent clowns, who tended to have begun by simply transferring their expertise in other fields to the screen, Keaton was a movie comic from the outset. Camera trickery, something Chaplin and, later, Laurel and Hardy rarely used, became a staple of Keaton's films: not that he used trickery to cheat, and he certainly never used it when he could do it for real, even if at risk to limb or, on occasion, life; rather, he recognized the camera's value in creating special effects which enhanced his films and delighted his audiences.

This new stage in Buster's career was speedily interrupted by America's involvement in World War I, where he served in the trenches and also became an entertainer, working in Europe to such good effect that it was 1919 before the army allowed him to get back into the movie swim. His return was timely, for Arbuckle had moved to Paramount for a series of features; Schenck therefore put Buster straight in as his new leading comic. He made *The Saphead* (1920) and then began a series of shorts and features which established him as a major star, a comic talent to rival Chaplin, and a film technician without serious rival.

Like Chaplin, Keaton was a genius but of a different order. His was a brilliant, if wayward, talent for technical perfection allied to a gift for original and inventive thought unparalleled in the development of silent comedy sight gags.

The technique of Keaton's best work is a key factor. Unlike Laurel and Hardy, at whom the audience has to look carefully to observe the workings of the comic mind, with Keaton it is there for all to see, admire and wonder at.

The features that Buster made from 1923 onwards included many that remain unchallengeable and enduring masterpieces: among them were *The Three Ages* (1923) (in which Oliver Hardy appeared), which was a parody of D. W. Griffith's *Intolerance* (1916), *Our Hospitality* (1923), *Sherlock Jr., The Navigator* (both 1924), *The General* (1927) and *Steamboat Bill Jr.* (1928). In many of his films Buster collaborated with Clyde Bruckman, who received writing and directing credits.

In later years Bruckman disclaimed much credit, implying that it was all really Buster's work. That this came at a time when Buster's fortunes, health and state of mind were at a very low ebb suggests that this may have been a display of

Buster Keaton is unimpressed by the Boys' serenading.

reciprocal loyalty towards a man who was always loyal to his friends. Certainly Bruckman's role cannot be overlooked for, despite the fact that Buster was unquestionably the presiding genius, retaining firm control over what was done in his films (to say nothing of the total physical commitment he applied), his films are demonstrably a team effort.

In the film world of Buster Keaton there were always mighty forces against which the small, unsmiling, stoic hero was obliged to struggle. Sometimes they were women but most often they were man-made artefacts like boats and trains and buildings. On memorable occasions it was also the elements against which Buster battled. In *One Week* (1920) the house he is transporting gets stuck on the railroad tracks; in *The Navigator* he tries single-handedly to tow an ocean-going liner from a rowing boat; in *Steamboat Bill Jr.* he manages to keep his feet during a hurricane which blows away buildings.

Keaton's deadpan approach to much of his work, allied to his bleak, sometimes black, humour, puzzled some people and was perhaps why Keaton always ran a poor third in popularity to Chaplin and Lloyd, his great rivals; moreover he had entered films later than them. With Buster, it was not always clear whether something was meant to be funny or should be taken seriously. More significant is that Keaton's major films came after 1923, by which time both Chaplin and Lloyd had enjoyed almost a decade of film-making (and in Chaplin's case, of massive success).

'Think slow, act fast,' Keaton averred, and much of the manner of his work cleaves to this maxim. (By contrast, Stan Laurel can be said to have thought slow and acted slower.) The sources of his comedy varied greatly. Most of the gags in *The Navigator* evolved out of the ship itself (a genuine ocean liner which Buster bought when he learned it was about to be scrapped). In *The Playhouse* (1921) he was temporarily incapacitated due to a broken leg and was therefore limited in his choice of physical gags. He set the opening sequence in a theatre and used a form of multiple-exposure photography to play all the roles in a minstrel show and the audience. (This device has been repeated often since, but not bettered, by many different performers, especially on television, which with all its advanced technology can cope easily with the procedures involved.) Later in the film, Keaton proves remarkably agile in his ape impersonation.

Aware that despite the virtual free hand and large budget given him by Schenck he trailed behind his two great rivals, Buster tried inserting pathos (an ingredient of Chaplin's films that Lloyd also attempted to use) but only rarely succeeded. In *Go West* (1925) the character he plays, Friendless, develops a truly affectionate companionship with Brown Eyes, a cow. Perhaps intending to parody Chaplin's *The Kid* (1921), in which the Little Fellow befriends pint-sized Jackie Coogan, Buster achieves here a superb balance between comedy and pathos.

Keaton's string of hits and especially the success of *Battling Butler* (1926) led to a massively budgeted movie which proved to be a financial flop. Perversely, as so often happened in Hollywood, the new film, *The General*, was a masterpiece that stands today as a testimony to one of the greatest comic talents the world has known.

What was 'wrong' with *The General* was its rich complexity, a densely textured story with elements of drama befitting a story set in the American Civil War and which includes scenes of soldiers dying. Such a form of comedy was not for 1927 audiences, nor indeed for those of the next few decades.

The stature of *The General*, and of Keaton, has grown in recent years and it is an unfortunate irony that at the time of its failure the effect was for Joe Schenck to cut back on the budget for the next film. In *College* (1927), Schenck insisted that the work should more closely echo the known success formula being demonstrated in the work of Harold Lloyd. It did not work, because Buster was not made to be a copyist and his work began to suffer.

By this time, too, his private life was in poor shape. He had married Natalie Talmadge in 1921 and thus became a member of one of filmdom's leading families. Natalie's sisters were Norma, a major silent star who was married to Joe Schenck, and Constance, who achieved almost as great a level of fame and popularity. (In 1919 members of the senior class at Princeton were solemnly reported by the press to have voted for their five favourite actresses: Norma came top with Constance taking fourth place.) Neither of the sisters succeeded in making the transition to talkies but in their heydays they were fabulously rich and lived the life of the movie star to the hilt. (It was

Norma Talmadge who, after her retirement, turned upon a crowd of autograph-hunters and cried, 'Go away, go away! I don't need you any more.') The girls' mother, Peg Talmadge, is supposed to have provided the inspiration for the character of Lorelei Lee in Anita Loos's book *Gentlemen Prefer Blondes*. In contrast to her fun-loving and somewhat scandalous sisters, Natalie was quiet, almost subdued, and appeared perfectly happy to live her life outside the limelight. In practice, her life with Buster proved to be anything but quiet and despite two children theirs was soon a marriage in name only. Buster sought companionship elsewhere, drinking with cronies and having affairs with several women (including Mae Busch, before she became a fixture in the screen world of Laurel and Hardy). In time the drinking led to alcoholism, which contributed towards his decline.

But Buster never lost sight of the fact that it was through Fatty Arbuckle that he had got his start in pictures or that as a result of Arbuckle's move to another studio he, Keaton, had been given leading roles by Schenck. Loyalty was a notable characteristic of Buster's and during the Arbuckle trial he volunteered to testify as a character witness. Although he and other stars were deterred by their studios, which were afraid of bad publicity, Arbuckle's lawyer turned him down, observing that a parade of Hollywood stars in the witness box might prove detrimental to his client's case.

When the trial was over Hollywood appeared to wash its hands of Arbuckle, but Buster set up a deal which ensured that his friend received a substantial percentage of the profits on all future Keaton pictures. These payments continued until Arbuckle's death in 1933. The apparent abandonment of Arbuckle by Hollywood was largely a cosmetic operation. As Tom Dardis has detailed in his biography of Keaton, six companies – Metro, Paramount, Universal, Goldwyn, Schenck and Educational – jointly established a company named Reel Comedies Inc., which employed Arbuckle to work as a director under an assumed name.

If the critical and financial disaster of *The General* had happened at any other time events might have taken a different course – even with Buster's now serious drinking problem. But it happened in 1927, when talkies were about to revolutionize Hollywood. Silent moviemakers of all kinds, including the comics, were worrying over what to do and how best to do it, and the purse-string holders naturally needed the assurance of stability in the new movie world. Buster, freely associating with other women, despite living under the same roof as Natalie (who at the urging of her family had long since ended her sexual relationship with Buster), and drinking heavily, raised questions; Keaton, maker of an expensive flop, gave the questioners their answers. From this moment on, control of his work passed from his hands into those of lesser and not always compatible spirits.

Undoubtedly suffering from the constraints under which it was made, *College* failed too, but while distinctly inferior to *The General* it did not really deserve its failure. It was inadequately promoted, as if everyone was aware that with talkies around the corner there were better things to do.

Steamboat Bill, Jr. was a brilliant exercise in technical virtuosity, intermingled with scenes in a theatre in which many examples of the vaudevillean's trade, which Buster knew so well from his youth, are shown. Later, a cyclone demolishes a building in front of which Buster stands motionless. In one of the (rightly) most famous moments in all cinema, the entire façade (some two tons in weight) falls forward, neatly framing Buster in the attic window opening. Yet, despite its evident quality, this film, too, failed financially.

Joe Schenck now decided to pull out of independent production and Buster signed with MGM, where Joe's brother Nick was in charge. Buster thought he would be his own boss; but as Stan Laurel was to discover when he and Oliver Hardy joined Fox and MGM, that was not how the major studios functioned. Of them all, MGM, where, so its advertising claimed, there were 'more stars than there are in heaven', had had least experience with comics. They did not understand Buster, he did not understand them and thus the decline into ordinariness and eventual obscurity began. It was not, therefore, simply the talkies which ended the success of Buster Keaton but rather extraneous events the effects of which were exacerbated by the advent of sound.

Eventually the film world realized that in Buster Keaton it had had, but let go, a comic genius whose stature continues to grow as the years pass, but by then he was an old man with too little time left in which to enjoy the late acclaim and the deserved renewal of his fame and popularity.

The fact that Harold Lloyd's films were so successful that they earned much more than Keaton's and only a little less than Chaplin's is a statistic requiring qualification. Quantity was a significant factor. Lloyd steadily made two films a year during the years of competition, while Keaton's production was erratic and Chaplin's pace was often positively lethargic.

The appeal of Harold Lloyd to audiences of the day is not easy to understand at first glance. Unlike Chaplin and so many others, he did not disguise himself as a 'character', although he tried enough such tricks before he evolved the style that led to his great popularity. When he began making comedies for Hal Roach there was no simply definable character. Almost one hundred films later he was no further on. Well, he had advanced a little: he had begun wearing horn-rimmed glasses. The breakthrough, when it came, was unexpected, giving rise to a unique screen comic.

Lloyd, who was born in 1893, began film work as an extra as early as 1912. Two years later he met Hal Roach, who was just about to form his own production company. Soon Lloyd was play-ing comic leads – Willie Work was his character's name – but with no success. After a spell with Mack Sennett he returned to Roach, having laboriously devised a character, Lonesome Luke, based upon clothes which contrasted sharply and deliberately with Chaplin's: too small instead of too big. However, as Walter Kerr has astutely observed, the development of Lloyd's characters, even the final successful one, was an entirely rational process in which he painstakingly, and, judging from the years it took to get it right, somewhat ineffectually struggled to work things out.

Lloyd acquired the horn-rimmed glasses in 1917 but was still unsure how they suited his energetic and sometimes violent screen character. What Lloyd *was* sure about was that somehow, some day, he would succeed. He set about ensur-ing his success not like a Chaplin or a Keaton, not like any other screen comic (or, for that matter, any dramatic actor), but like a careful, dedicated and occasionally ruthless businessman.

He reasoned that to be successful he had to be known, very well-known, to movie theatre audi-ences, and that meant he had to make lots of films. To achieve this he made exploratory one-reelers while continuing his two-reelers. This way, he could make more films, ensure he maintained production schedules and guarantee the film bookers that there would never be any shortage of supply. He maintained his plan, using the glasses partly so that he was readily recognized and partly to contrast a studious appearance with energetic behaviour, and using gags without understanding what made some work and others not. As Kerr observes, Lloyd 'was still following the blueprint of a joke without having grasped what it was meant to house.'

In the 1920s Lloyd entered feature film-making with the same practical thoroughness that had marked his earlier strivings. He decided that the longer format was where the future lay and adjusted his production schedule accordingly, although in *Grandma's Boy* (1922) the film, begun as a two-reeler, just grew. In this film he adopted the character he was to retain for the rest of his career. Harold (the name his character now always bore) is a mild-mannered, clean-cut boy who does not want to fight but if goaded beyond endurance will ruthlessly strike down the evil-doer. He was virtuous, but he was also virile. In short, he became an American as Americans perceived themselves.

His subsequent and highly successful features, which included *Safety Last* (1923) and *The Fresh-man* (1925), confirmed that he had finally arrived at the right formula. They also gave him inde-pendence, that elusive grail for which so many silent clowns strove.

Harold Lloyd's chosen form of comedy was heavily dependent upon the excitement of audi-ences seeing their reflected selves in dangerous situations. It often appeared that the thrills were achieved at great personal risk for Lloyd. He was not, however, as meticulous in creating the struc-ture of his gags as was Keaton, nor as determined as Buster to refrain from camera trickery. On occasion, however, he went to remarkable lengths to 'show' that there was no faking. Yet there was.

In *Safety Last* his climb up the side of a multi-storey building was filmed partly on a structure mounted on top of a real building but facing inwards so that if he (or stuntman Harvey Parry) fell, the drop was only fifteen feet and even then on to mattresses. On shots which showed a man on a real skyscraper more than a hundred feet above the ground, it was Harvey Parry.

Harold Lloyd, careful, dedicated and occasionally ruthless.

Careful angling of the camera and skilful editing allowed Lloyd to 'cheat' his public but his view was simple: if he was making a movie to thrill his audience then thrill them he would and to the very best of his ability – even if that entailed camera-fakery. Nevertheless, Lloyd turned himself into an acrobat. If his acrobatic skills were never in the same class as Keaton's, they elicit great admiration simply because he worked so hard to acquire them.

By 1927, with talkies about to change the face of popular entertainment, Lloyd was bringing important qualities to his films. In that year he made *The Kid Brother*, which is visually delightful and shows far more concern for the pictorial values of film than the work of many of Lloyd's counterparts. More than most, he appeared best poised for the transition to talkies. But Lloyd was growing tired of the movies and was not enjoying film-making as much as he had in the past. Financially, he was completely secure. He owned the rights to many of the hundreds of films he had made, certainly to all the important ones. He was married to Mildred Davis, who had appeared in some of his films and who remained his wife until her death in 1969, and he had numerous outside interests. He made some good talkies, including *Feet First* (1930), *Movie Crazy* (1932), *The Cat's Paw* (1934) and *The Milky Way* (1936), but the spark and enthusiasm were gone. In 1938, after completing *Professor Beware*, he drifted quietly into contented retirement.

In 1947 he emerged briefly in order to make *The Sins of Harold Diddlebock* but did not pursue the comeback trail. Only in the 1960s did he realize the value of the films he owned: the resulting two compilations brought him to the attention of a new generation of moviegoers and regenerated the enthusiasm of his old fans. Like Buster Keaton, Harold Lloyd, who died in 1971, also lived long enough to enjoy much deserved late acclaim.

None of the other silent clowns approached Chaplin, Keaton and Lloyd in either quality or popularity.

Harry Langdon had a varied career and draws a mixed response today. At his best he displayed certain characteristics in common with Chaplin and with Stan Laurel, with whom he shared the status of archetypal ineffectual. His bathetic little character failed to expand upon the original but the main reason for Langdon's eventual failure

was that he mistook bathos for pathos and childishness for behaving like a child. Moreover, when Langdon sought sympathy from his audience he discovered a wide and artificial gulf of his own making. He was not a man with child-like traits (as were Laurel and Hardy), neither was he a man (as were Chaplin, Keaton and Lloyd), nor was he even a blank-faced clown (as was Larry Semon). He was instead a child, and a not very bright one either, in a man's body. His childishness prevented the audience's response from being very deep. Most adults soon weary of childishness, even from children (and even their own); childishness in a man is at best irritating and at worst embarrassing or mildly distasteful.

The decline of Langdon's career, coming as it did when he insisted on taking over as director of his own films, precipitated claims that he was very much a puppet in the hands of his directors, especially Frank Capra. In Langdon's case these views appear to have been better substantiated than the claims and counterclaims which surround the 'creation' of Laurel and Hardy. Nevertheless, Langdon continued making films (some shorts with Roach in 1929-30) and worked regularly throughout the 1930s, occasionally as a gag writer on some Laurel and Hardy films. As noted earlier, he also played opposite Oliver Hardy in *Zenobia*. He died in 1944, aged 60.

Larry Semon, with whom Oliver Hardy had worked extensively (Stan Laurel, too, worked with Semon), kept silent film comedy much closer to the great tradition of the mime artist, not least with his white-face make-up (even without make-up Semon is still remarkably clown-like). Despite some financial flops, resulting as much from overspending in production as through any absence of quality, he might well have proved to be a challenger to the great triumvirate. Unfortunately, however, the failures drove him out of films and back into vaudeville shortly before he died, in 1928 at the age of 39.

The reasons for the relative lack of success of those silent clowns who tried talkies and features vary, therefore, from one case to another. For some, sound was no help at all and, as Chaplin's case shows, was probably feared. For others, as Keaton's career demonstrates, the problem was that the big studios failed to comprehend ability and worth. In Lloyd's case it was simply a matter of weariness and a decision to take-the-money-and-run to a happy retirement. For all of them, the transition from short film to feature was perhaps a greater difficulty, requiring a different approach from the free-flowing gag routines upon which their early successes were based.

The silent two-reeler, running for 25 or even 30 minutes, and the three-reel sound film, lasting 25 minutes, were ideally suited to a series of developed sight gags which could have a logical beginning, middle and end. The longer format usually resulted in what was for all practical purposes three or more two-reelers linked, often not very convincingly, by a tenuous plot (or kept apart by even less convincing sub-plots). Few, if any, of those concerned with the business of film-making realized the problem before it was too late and these great comic talents had foundered,

grown old, faded into obscurity, or simply died.

By 1940 Laurel and Hardy, if not kings, like Chaplin, Keaton and Lloyd, then certainly crown princes of comedy, had proved conclusively that sound was no problem and, with a few uncertainties along the way, they had come as close as any to meeting the challenge of feature films. Their imminent move to a major studio presented no obvious problems.

They approached this new stage in their careers with their screen personas solidly established and a formidable and enviable array of technical abilities founded in long experience of film-making and, in Laurel's case, years of success on the boards. Their technique and style are therefore worthy of some examination.

CHAPTER EIGHT

Me and My Pal
Style, Technique and Influence

'What is comedy? I don't know. Does anybody?'
Stan Laurel

When asked by John McCabe to define comedy even Stan Laurel could not find an answer. If he could not, then who can?

Describing the techniques of film comedy may be slightly easier than trying to discover what makes people laugh but is, in the end, just as fruitless.

In the case of Laurel and Hardy their technique shows so little, if at all, that describing it becomes harder than ever – yet, perversely perhaps, the reward for doing so is greater than, say, in the case of Keaton. In Keaton's work the technique is much more readily apparent and this, too, can improve the appreciation of a good sight gag. The scrupulous timing of Keaton's rope swing across a waterfall and, for another example, the collapse of a house around his ears (both sequences impeccably edited) draw respectful admiration in equal proportion to the laugh each generates. When Stan and Ollie simultaneously pull the wheels off a stationary automobile, causing it to lurch forward like a poleaxed steer, the mechanics of the gag – technically impossible after all – are lost in the laugh. The timing of the delayed ending to a gag (waiting for the last brick of a collapsing chimney to fall on Ollie's head, for example) would be polished to perfection by the film's editing, a task most often performed by Stan.

The philosophical view that science grew out of art and that the dividing line remains permanently blurred is nowhere better demonstrated than in silent film comedy. In the case of Laurel and Hardy that already hazy borderline becomes so faint that it has led many otherwise astute observers to suggest that they had no technique.

Nothing could be further from the truth; their work was so good that the blending of the technical needs of film-making with the desire to make people laugh became seamless.

Much of their success in achieving this lies in the development of the on-screen personas of Stan and Ollie, which enabled their comic style to grow naturally.

Stan and Ollie on-screen are no more mean-spirited than the off-screen Stan and Babe. As Ernie Wise says, 'You knew they were nice people . . . you were comfortable with them.' But on-screen they added extra qualities which attracted their audiences. Not least was the manner in which they responded to the deals fate dealt them. Good luck, not that it happened often, was accepted gratefully, if with the mild uncertainty of someone who does not believe he really deserves it; bad luck, which for Stan and Ollie usually came in catastrophic proportions, was never the fault of outside agencies – they gamely took the blame upon their own shoulders. If fate wanted them to fall into a neck-high hole or cannon off a rooftop, then they must have done something wrong otherwise it would not have happened to them. An additional and important element in the maintenance of their relationship with one another is that while they might blame one another for the immediate catastrophe ('Here's another nice mess . . .') this would never last beyond the heat of the moment.

With such responses they were already well on their way to being likeable. Moreover, they possessed qualities which audiences recognized in themselves and in others of their acquaintance.

Stan was forever timidly uncertain. He always hesitated to open a cupboard door because he knew that with his luck something would probably fall out and hit him. But he opened the door anyway, and something usually fell out and hit him . . . except, of course, when it hit Ollie. In such moments, when the audience knew just as well as the hapless Stan that something awful was about to happen, the Boys showed a perfect grasp of the technique of comic anticipation. And the audiences laughed even more for having been proved right in their expectations. Also, for the moment, they were brighter than the person in the movie. The fact that Stan, on-screen, was dumber than the least of his audience was beside the point. For Stan, this was important and he never tried to outsmart his audience.

In his behaviour towards his fearful and hopelessly incompetent partner Ollie was commandingly rude. He bullied Stan unmercifully, but was unfailingly polite to others, especially figures in authority or of an apparently superior class. Ollie's on-screen behaviour towards women was impeccable, except in certain instances with his 'wives'. Ray Alan, who observed the Boys at close hand while working with them on their 1953-4 British tour, recalls: 'Babe was very much a Georgian gentleman. If a woman came into the room he would want to stand up, bad though his legs were. He always wanted to show respect. He was incredibly well-mannered; his screen gestures were all extended from his real self.'

Despite the seemingly unattractive characteristics Ollie displayed towards Stan, he was the one who most often drew a response approaching love from his audience. Perhaps it was the gestures, the manners, but most of all it was the roundness of the character. As Peter Barnes observed in his appreciation of the duo in *Films and Filming*, Ollie's 'sublime incompetence and mute appeals to the audience when defeated by the malice of inanimate objects endeared him to all the pure in heart. For behind the commanding worldly airs, the courtly bows, the ineffectual bluster, there beat a heart more innocent and childlike than his partner's. We were not fooled.'

The pair of them existed in a curiously quiet world – not just the world of the silent film, for even after the coming of sound there were often large pools of silence in Laurel and Hardy films. These were never the equivalent of the frequent *longueurs* which sometimes spoilt the films of

their less skilled colleagues. These lacunae contained the inaudible yet tangible working of Stan's brain as he bravely attempted to reason through the problem of the moment; they contained the similarly silent processes of Ollie's grey matter as he sought to understand why he, of all people, should have fallen foul of life's ingratitudes.

And these silent pools were filled, too, with the magical use of body language: Stan's snapped-string marionette walk and Ollie's courtly roll were often imitated but never completely mastered by others.

Facially, they used a small yet perfectly developed range of expressions, the best of which were offered full face to the camera and hence to the spectators who were thus transformed from voyeurs to, if not participants, at least the status of confidantes. Stan's blank-eyed look of uncertainty and Ollie's exasperated ruefulness helped bind performers to audience as none before and few since have achieved. True, many silent screen comics played to the camera, but even when Chaplin did it the gulf between screen image and movie-theatre audience was never fully bridged. Chaplin always remained aloof from the audience of little fellows his Little Fellow sought to reflect. Stan and Ollie never pretended to be like their audience – no one out there, they asserted, can be as dumb as we are – but audiences loved them the more for that implicit difference.

Among their small but perfected armoury of screencraft was Ollie's tie-twiddle, used at moments when he had brought embarrassment upon himself for committing some small sin (often one of imperfectly grasped etiquette). Then there was his way of signing his name: a prefatory series of flourishes worthy of a sixteenth-century courtier and a concluding full stop which stabs through the document. And while such activity took place the derby, as often as not, was removed from his head to lie gently upon his arm.

Stan would use his sticking-up hair as a means of indicating or exaggerating his fear and stupidity, while his general inability to carry out the simplest action was demonstrated by his abject failure even to manage to fold his arms. And, of course, there was his cry: a face-wrinkling escape into child-like behaviour which stopped a small but superbly well-judged step short of descending into idiocy.

Laurel and Hardy portrayed themselves as eternal optimists who expected to succeed in a world that demonstrated time after time that they really had no business being there in the first place. Mostly, they took their comeuppances stoically, as their audiences had to take theirs. Yet both could, and regularly did, turn on those who sought to humiliate them (and Laurel and Hardy were *never* humiliated), in a destructive assault in which they clearly revelled. Their audiences loved that too, because here for a moment, however vicariously, they could kick back at whoever was subjecting them to similar torment. When, therefore, in the final section of *You're Darn Tootin'*, the Boys fall out and kick and punch one another furiously, it is only a prelude to a general orgy of kicking and punching and, eventually, trouser-ripping which spreads to encompass a streetful of men, who initially represent those who would rule the rest of the herd. That they are abruptly turned into a herd themselves is effectively counter-pointed when the Boys depart, as friendly towards one another as ever – indeed, having debagged an extremely fat man, they share a pair of pants.

This ending, with the Boys exiting peacefully, illustrates an important quality of their work: they do not really mean to cause anyone any harm. As the distinguished documentary film-maker John Grierson pointed out in a 1931 essay in *Everyman*, Laurel and Hardy 'deplore the disturbance they are creating. They hate it, and would avoid it if they could. They are men of peace. But in this case the meek are not blessed. They do not inherit the earth. They inherit chaos.'

Yet for all the chaos and clamour of their lives, there was an all-pervading sense of gentleness. Ray Alan has commented:

I remember seeing a compilation of their films at the end of which the narrator said, 'Two very funny gentlemen . . . two very funny, gentle, men.' And that is what they were, in their work and in their private selves. They had no malice, no cruelty. Babe told me, 'That was Stan. Stan insisted on taking the pain out of comedy. Like that scene where we're at the top of the stairs and I trip over the bags. You see Stan looking, and you hear me: Ooohhh! Cut! Next thing you see is me sitting at the bottom of the stairs, obviously unhurt, giving the look to the camera. That was Stan. The first thing was, Don't show the fall, that's cruel, it's funnier when you only imagine it. But, when you *do* see, you're not hurt. We were cartoons, we always came back; we tore our fur off but we always came back in the next scene with our fur back on. That's the way Stan wanted to do it.'

As has already been noted, here and elsewhere, most particularly by John McCabe in his invaluable studies of the duo, Stan Laurel's role in the making of their films was crucial. Inherent in the films' construction is the need to build a gag logically and, indeed, to build a film logically (even if that logic occasionally crumbled). To accomplish this their early films were made in sequence – by no means uncommon practice at the time. Later, with the longer films over which Stan had no real control, film-making procedures had altered irrevocably and this could no longer be done.

At the Guardian Lecture in London in October 1986, Hal Roach, then 94 years of age, remarked that Stan was a great gagman but did not have the capacity to build an entire film. If Roach is right, even if Stan had controlled all their feature films they might still have lacked coherent construction. Yet the superior quality of *Our Relations* and *Way Out West* offers persuasive evidence to the contrary.

The continuity of the early films and the manner in which the ultimate chaos grew from very simple beginnings by logical progression cannot be put down to chance. As Jesse Bier observes in *The Rise and Fall of American Humor*, 'Since much of the American mentality itself battens on simplification – on clichés, on shibboleths, on proverbs, on slogans, on formulas – an equal amount of [American] humour is in the service of unholy complication.'

Most people *do* think in clichés, not with originality, wit, inventiveness or brilliance. Most comics also think in clichés. But in the early Laurel and Hardy films there is a highly inventive comic mind at work. Whether that mind was one man's or a blending of two minds or was a collective intelligence, whether it understood the philosophy of what it was doing or simply grasped it intuitively, we may never know. But time after time it makes itself apparent.

Most of all, however, it is that spirit of togetherness suffusing their work that makes the comic style of Laurel and Hardy so effective. Neither claimed the audience's attention to the detriment of the other. While accepting that Stan Laurel was the creative driving force, Ernie Wise considers that Oliver Hardy was the better, more versatile performer, not least for the manner in which he projected his partner – either by an overt look at the camera or through the many subtle touches and gestures which pervade their films.

Roy Castle's view of their togetherness likens it to a family. Perhaps they did fight all the time but, like that of brothers and sisters, the fighting was only on the surface. Underneath they loved one another – and woe betide any outsider who ventured into the fray, for that would instantly unify the squabblers.

Ray Alan has no doubt that Stan's was a brilliant comic mind. On tour in 1954, he recalls that Stan would stand in the wings every night when he was on . . .

. . . when *anyone* was on, and would watch the performance. When you came off he'd say, 'Come and see me in my dressing room. I got an idea.' Later, he'd explain, pointing out that when I'd do this, and then do that, I should wait. 'You're killing the laugh for yourself. You know, you should get two laughs. You do this, hold it there and you get a laugh, then you go on and get a second laugh.' He was absolutely right and there was no question of saying, try something and if if didn't work, sorry! It worked. It was right. He was so analytical, he could just look at a piece and say, 'That should come out, put this over there,' and so on. He was unbelievable. I get laughs today with techniques I learned from Stan Laurel.

None of the other comic film duos of their day had the particular qualities that Laurel and Hardy demonstrated, although several tried to compete. Once the great success of Laurel and Hardy was observed in Hollywood other pairs of male comics emerged. The most obvious contenders for their crown, Abbott and Costello, had begun making films in 1940, when, coincidentally, Laurel and Hardy were reaching the end of their road with Hal Roach.

Bud Abbott (the tall, aggressive one) and Lou Costello (the fat, tormented one) began working together in vaudeville in the late 1920s. When they came to national radio (in 1938) and films they had a series of established and well-polished routines. Some of these – their sketch 'Who's On First?' is perhaps the best-known example – were unsurpassed examples of the fast patter routine. Since talking pictures were a long-established fact by the time of their movie début, Abbott and Costello did not have to learn many new tricks. There was no need for them to learn new sight gags. Neither were they especially original. The sight gags they were obliged to use from time to time were, as often as not, borrowed from earlier comedies made by others. Partially to blame for this was their gag-man Clyde Bruckman, who can be excused some of the pilfering from Keaton's films since he had had a hand in developing them in the first place. Their chase sequences drew upon Lou's early work as a stuntman (he was also an extra in Laurel and Hardy's *Battle of the Century*), but were frequently clumsy and could not be described as inventive. Such sequences apart, they went right on doing what they had always done and for all practical purposes they carried on doing it until their partnership ended.

What this meant in the long term was that their essentially cardboard cut-out characters, which worked so well on the stage and on radio, failed to attract the same kind of following as Laurel and Hardy: not that Bud and Lou lacked a following at the time – far from it, for they were a staggering success. Neither they nor the studio which brought them to the screen saw any reason to tinker with something that was already well-proven. Consequently, they never developed real characters with whom the audience could identify or whom they would grow to love. Indeed, love was not a word which even their most ardent fan could use to define any aspect of their work. They certainly gave no indication of even liking, let alone loving, one another.

Most different from Laurel and Hardy, however, were the pace and the noise level at which Abbott and Costello worked. They were brash, noisy and aggressive, like the times in which they rose to the top. The quiet, reflective qualities of Laurel and Hardy were just one of many past ideas that were being junked wholesale by all branches of the entertainment industry. New might not have been better than old, but at least it *was* new.

Although Abbott and Costello moved into TV with some success there was again no noticeable change in their style, or in the noise level. In 1957, two years before Lou Costello's death, the partnership broke up.

Bert Wheeler and Robert Woolsey were single comics who were formed into a team by Florenz Ziegfeld for his 1928 Broadway show *Rio Rita*. The following year a film version was made in which Wheeler and Woolsey also appeared. Thereafter they appeared in a succession of films of variable quality but never attained the following their strong line in verbal humour deserved. In appearance Wheeler and Woolsey bore a marked resemblance to Ernie Wise and Eric Morecambe (even to the glasses) although Woolsey's main trademark was a George Burns-like cigar. In some of their films they were directed by George Stevens, by then graduated from cameraman on early Laurel and Hardy films. The quality of Wheeler and Woolsey's work declined sharply in the mid-1930s and they made their last film together in 1937, the year before Robert Woolsey's death. Bert Wheeler reverted to working as a single and made films into the 1950s before turning to TV and cabaret work.

The artificial creation of a comedy duo was not a prerogative of the Broadway stage. RKO did it in the movies in 1944 with Wally Brown and Alan Carney in a direct attempt to counter the box-office inroads being made by Universal's Abbott and Costello. Their career was as patchy as their films and by 1946 RKO had abandoned the idea.

The anarchic routines of Olsen and Johnson had more in common with the Marx Brothers' than those of any of the comic duos, while the later teaming of Dean Martin and Jerry Lewis never made any serious attempt to create a double-act in the real sense of the term. Neither of these acts, of course, owed anything whatsoever to Laurel and Hardy.

Of the more recent double-acts on TV only that of Morecambe and Wise shows any obvious relationship to Laurel and Hardy, and then only in the duo's earlier performances. At the very beginning, however, they based their joint style (both had worked as single acts before teaming up) on Abbott and Costello. As Ernie Wise says, this gave them two lives. In the early part they were more like Lou and Bud, straight man and comic: 'Then later on [we] became more like Laurel and Hardy, two comics.' A routine from a 1960s TV show demonstrates this: Eric Morecambe, dressed very unconvincingly as Mark Antony, enters carrying Ernie, who is even less convincing as the corpse of Julius Caesar. As Eric delivers the funeral oration Ernie begins to slip from his grasp and the next five minutes use many of the techniques displayed in Stan's attempts to lift Ollie through a window in 'Scram!'. Later on, of course, Morecambe and Wise ceased to be copyists and evolved their own style.

The list of individual performers who have drawn, consciously or unconsciously, from Laurel and Hardy is not only innumerable but also enormously wide in range. There are numerous references to routines created by the Boys in the Blake Edwards-Peter Sellers Pink Panther films and, indeed, Edwards dedicated The Great Race (1965) to Laurel and Hardy. His 1986 film A Fine Mess (starring Ted Danson and Howie Mandel) appears to have aimed at the creation of a comic partnership which mirrored Stan and Ollie. In the event it missed by a mile.

The American TV star Dick Van Dyke, whose early show-business career included a spell as a mime artist, incorporated many of Stan Laurel's techniques into his own performances, becoming along the way a close friend of Stan's. In the circumstances, Van Dyke's leading role in the graceless Carl Reiner movie The Comic (1969), reputedly inspired by the lives of Buster Keaton and Stan, can best be described as misguided.

Even the world of the cartoon film borrowed from the Boys. Philip Sheard, an admirer of their work, has compiled a list of some 30 cartoon subjects, ranging from Mickey Mouse to Popeye, which have incorporated Laurel and Hardy into their artificial worlds.

The question of copying from a good original was very much in the air when Laurel and Hardy joined Twentieth Century-Fox after the dissolution of their long relationship with Hal Roach. Uncomfortably aware of the competition of Abbott and Costello, the studio was determined to beat them at their own game. In so doing they completely overlooked one obvious fact: that in Laurel and Hardy they already had original comic talent that could easily out-perform Abbott and Costello. Also, in Stan Laurel, they had someone who could out-think pretty well anyone then working in film comedy. It was a mistake that cost the studio money. It also cost Laurel and Hardy their film careers.

CHAPTER NINE

Nothing But Trouble

The Big Studio Years

'What was there for us to do but get out?'
Stan Laurel

Between leaving Roach and reporting for their first film for a big studio Stan and Babe fulfilled an ambition to appear again before live audiences. For about three months they toured the United States with *The Laurel and Hardy Revue* and followed this with a spin through the Caribbean playing to the Armed Forces. By the time they had done with this they were eager to return to the screen.

When the Boys joined Twentieth Century-Fox in 1941 it was with the greatest of expectations. They had formed their own production company, Laurel and Hardy Feature Productions, but, lacking capital, were obliged to go to one or another of the major studios. Stan had many new ideas for improving upon old and well-loved formulae; both he and Babe were ready, willing and keen to enter a new phase of their career. Looked at from the outside there was no reason to suspect that this would not crown all their previous glories. With any real awareness of the studio system in Hollywood at the time, and, of course, with the benefit of hindsight, it is plain to see that they never stood a chance.

In no area of film-making in Hollywood was the role of the money men, be they private investors, bankers, 'the New York office' or simply the accountants, more in control than in the major studios. Given the huge sums of money which were needed to make movies as production techniques became steadily more complex, it was inevitable that costs had to be closely budgeted. To achieve this the people needed to control expenditure were drawn from the appropriate professions. Almost without exception, this meant that values relating to the artistic, creative and inventive side of moviemaking often came low on the list of priorities. One effect of tight budgeting resulted in the major studios establishing relatively rigid systems of operation which left no room for free spirits. In the case of many of the moviemakers who had learned their trade in the freewheeling days of the silents, this proved to be a hardship, and especially so in the case of the great silent comics.

When the Boys reported to Fox for their first film, *Great Guns* (1941), they quickly found that here they were no more than any hired hand. They were given lines to speak, scenes to play and that was all. For Stan Laurel, the realization that he would not be allowed to contribute to the content of their work was shattering. Years later the bitterness and hurt still showed when Stan reflected on their experiences to his friend and biographer John McCabe. 'We had no say in those films,' he observed, 'and it sure looked it.'

Quite simply, they had been placed in the hands of people who did not understand the kind of humour at which the Boys excelled. They saw the surface and failed to observe that what made Stan and Ollie funny was not the gag, not the funny line, but the manner in which they approached each situation, the way in which they responded. The studio people failed to grasp the fact that what made Stan and Ollie the funniest comedy duo of all time was the depth and strength of their characterizations. If they were put into gags which depended upon something other than those characters, the laugh could result from the situation alone; in such situations Laurel

Soldier . . .

. . . *Boys in* Great Guns.

Dining out with Mantan Moreland in A-Haunting We Will Go.

and Hardy were no funnier than any two people drawn at random from the ranks of comics or comic actors. In many of the scenes Fox gave them to play, even straight actors would have been as funny – or as unfunny.

In *Great Guns* the Boys sign up for the army in order to be with their boss, the millionaire Dan Forrester (Dick Nelson), but quickly fall foul of Sergeant Hippo (Edmund MacDonald). Also along for the experience is Penelope, the Boys' pet crow, an inductee guaranteed to upset the sergeant. When their boss falls for a local girl, Ginger (Sheila Ryan), Stan and Ollie, afraid that she's after Dan's money, try to put a stop to their affair. Later, discovering that Ginger is really the right girl for Dan, they patch things up for the young couple. Dan shows his appreciation by rescuing the Boys when they are captured by the other side during manoeuvres.

Among the bit-part players in the film is diminutive Alan Ladd, who was already in the eighth year of his ten-year struggle to make the grade in pictures.

Apart from a leaden script and turgid direction, there are two main problems with *Great Guns*. One is that Laurel and Hardy are simply not allowed to be inventively funny but are obliged to re-use, without improvement, old jokes – the only merit of which is that they were, at least, pinched from their own old movies. The second is that the storyline and setting for the movie bear a marked resemblance to *Buck Privates*, which had been

released earlier in the year. This film, Abbott and Costello's second movie, was a huge hit. With it, the Boys' noisy, brash, extrovert competitors bounced way up the money-earning polls to third place; they also featured high in the popularity polls, and stayed there. After years of being not only the best but virtually the only duo regularly making movies, Laurel and Hardy were suddenly a poor second and, worse, seemingly making feeble copies of their new rivals' films.

Similarly, Abbott and Costello's *Hold That Ghost* (1941) was a forerunner to the Boys' second film at Fox, *A-Haunting We Will Go* (1942). Fortunately the quality picked up a little, but not much. The story starts promisingly enough with the Boys in their customary position: down on their luck. Threatened with jail unless they leave town, where they have been picked up as vagrants, Stan and Ollie answer a newspaper advertisement which offers a free train ride plus $50 for delivery of a package to Dayton, Ohio.

Alarmingly, the package turns out to be a coffin apparently containing the corpse of a recently deceased man. Faced with no alternative they take the job on and are soon on their way. Unfortunately, as the train is being loaded the Boys' casket is accidentally mishandled, leaving them with a box containing part of the impedimenta of Dante the Magician (Harry A. Jansen). Also on board is Dante's assistant, the lovely Margo (Sheila Ryan), and various other individuals including Mantan Moreland and Willie Best as a fearful black porter and a wide-eyed black waiter. (Such characters were almost required casting in any Hollywood comedy which featured coffins and corpses in the days before the rising tide of black consciousness drove such stereotypes from the screen.) Complicating the Boys' task still further is the fact that the coffin does not really hold a corpse – instead it is a temporary home for a gangster who is desperate to reach Dayton to collect an inheritance.

Soon separated from their money by a conman, the Boys are hired by Dante to help out with his act. This involves Ollie puffing at a magic flute, which is the only way of keeping in the air a rope which is Stan's only means of support. The gangster's aides arrive at the theatre to recover the right box only to be captured by federal agents aided and abetted by Stan and Ollie. The film closes with Stan falling victim to one of Dante's tricks – miniaturized inside a prop egg. Ollie

Schrecken aller Spione

Looking for bombs in Air Raid Wardens.

Overleaf: doing their bit for the war effort in The Tree in a Test Tube.

breaks it, finds his weeping pal and laughs uproariously.

For their next feature film Laurel and Hardy were temporarily released from the saltmine of Fox but their move over to MGM allowed them to fare only marginally better. This time they did have the benefit of a friendly face in the cast, or would have had if Edgar Kennedy had ever managed to look friendly on the screen. In *Air Raid Wardens* (1943) Stan and Ollie are trying to establish themselves in business in Huxton, a small town which benefits from an engineering plant producing chemicals for the war effort. Having failed at everything, the Boys are taken on as air-raid wardens. The local newspaperman, Dan Madison (Stephen McNally), and his girl-friend Peggy (Jacqueline White) are about the

only residents of Huxton happy to welcome them. During a mock raid, Stan and Ollie overcome the protests of some of those in town who dislike their presence by designating pompous banker J. P. Norton (Howard Freeman) a casualty and bandaging him to a makeshift stretcher. They then order moving man Joe Bledsoe (Kennedy) to carry out various menial tasks. His response is to crown them with a bottle. When the Boys are found unconscious with an empty bottle beside them they are fired. Later, during another test ordered by a visiting civil defence leader, the Boys counter an attempt to sabotage the chemical plant when they overhear a plot being hatched by local businessman Eustace Middling (Donald Meek) and a German agent.

There is a relative absence of staged gags in *Air*

Raid Wardens, which makes a tit-for-tat exchange between Stan, Ollie and Edgar Kennedy look a trifle forced. As if noting this as a possible means of changing direction, their return to Fox for their next picture found them cast in fairly straight-forward roles.

In a brief moment away from the lot (in fact it was during a lunch break) the Boys did their bit for the government. *The Tree in a Test Tube* (1943) is a colour film made for the Department of Agriculture. As the narrator explains, the Boys silently demonstrate the uses of timber and its by-products.

Jitterbugs (1943) finds Stan and Ollie down on their luck, as usual. They are musicians who meet con-man Chester Wright (Robert Bailey), who convinces them he can turn water into petrol with the aid of a wonderful new capsule. The Boys set up a stand at a local carnival playing music to attract the crowds before starting to sell their magic capsules. At this time they also meet up with a glamorous young woman named Susan Cowan (Vivian Blaine). When the locals discover

that the gasoline capsules are phony they form a mob but Chester reappears, pretends to be a sheriff and takes the Boys away with him in their trailer, in which Susan has been accidentally locked. When they learn that Susan has been conned out of thousands of dollars by a pair of swindlers, Stan, Ollie and Chester determine to help her. Stan dresses up as Susan's rich aunt while Ollie dons the garb of a rich Southern colonel, falling effortlessly into the appropriate and natural mannerisms, and they take on the con-men. They succeed in recovering Susan's money but fall prisoner to the swindlers on board a showboat. After a chase down-river in the boat, which has a mind of its own, the Boys are rescued by Chester and the police, on whose side they momentarily find themselves.

Jitterbugs was well produced and had the benefit of Vivian Blaine, an attractive blonde in the mould of the highly popular Betty Grable. In the 1950s she gained considerable acclaim on the stages of Broadway and London's West End in *Guys and Dolls* (and also appeared in the 1955 film version). The absence of the usual comic routines came as something of a blessing in *Jitterbugs* as the repetition, normally an endearing quality of Laurel and Hardy's work, had proved to be a burden even to their greatest fans since the dead hand of the major studios had fallen over them. The roles within roles, Stan's 'aunt' and Ollie's 'Southern gentleman', are delightful impersonations. Stan's occasional appearances in drag were sufficiently few and far between for them to be interesting and his thorough grasp of the fundamentals of music hall allowed him to carry off such deceptions with considerable aplomb. As for Ollie's portrayal of a Southern gentleman, he was doing that most difficult of tasks after all his years as a pompous dunce – he was playing himself.

The director of *Jitterbugs* was Malcolm St Clair, who had enjoyed a highly distinguished career in the silent era. In the mid-1920s his sophisticated comedies showed a sparkling yet delicate touch which allowed him to be fairly bracketed with Ernst Lubitsch. Unfortunately his star waned and the quality of his movies declined abruptly just before talkies came in. Nevertheless, he continued to direct but with none of his earlier touch of class. Of his late films, *Jitterbugs* was one of his better efforts. Alas for Laurel and Hardy, who would be directed again by St Clair, the spiral was still downwards.

Choosing partners for Jitterbugs.

Mal St Clair was also director for the *Dancing Masters* (1943), in which Stan once more appeared in drag, in a scene in which he wears a ballerina's costume. The Boys are operating the Arthur Hurry School of Dancing, where one of their students is a girl called Mary Harlan (Trudy Marshall) whose boyfriend, Grant (Robert Bailey), is heartily disliked by her parents. Grant is an inventor, but when Stan and Ollie demonstrate his latest device, a kind of ray gun, to Mary's father in the hope that he will finance its production they succeed only in burning down the family home. The Boys decide to back Grant themselves as soon as they can raise a large sum of money, which in their case means as long as it takes to teach Ollie how to *jeter*. However, there is one way whereby they might lay hands on some money. The Boys have recently been approached by gangsters (including Robert Mitchum) posing as insurance agents who have made an offer they can't refuse. With Stan's legs and other parts insured for several thousand dollars all Ollie needs do is arrange an accident. He employs a similar device to that used in *Battle of the Century*, a banana skin, but, being Ollie, when he finally succeeds in breaking a leg it is his own. The gangsters, whose insurance racket involves elimi-

Stan teaching the girls in The Dancing Masters.

Time for a toast between the terpsichory in The Dancing Masters.

nating their policy-holders and collecting the proceeds, are arrested.

The repetition of old gags, which abounds in Laurel and Hardy films, usually to good effect, was wearing thin by the time of *Dancing Masters*. Stan's polishing and revising had given way to an imposed and often clumsy re-use of old material. This might well have been a welcome moment for their contracts to be terminated, but Fox still had plans for more movies; the outcome shows that whatever planning took place it did not include intelligent use of the available talent.

The Big Noise (1944) found St Clair, who was fast losing what little grip he had left, once more seated in the director's chair. With a clearly uninterested Stan and Ollie, a weaker than usual script, and almost total reliance upon barely warmed-over gags from old movies (including the two-men-in-a-berth routine from *Berth Marks* 15 years earlier), this effort had no chance of revitalizing the team's flagging reputation. As Stan remarked to John McCabe, his request that they should modify the old sketch by setting it in an

With young Robert Mitchum in The Dancing Masters.

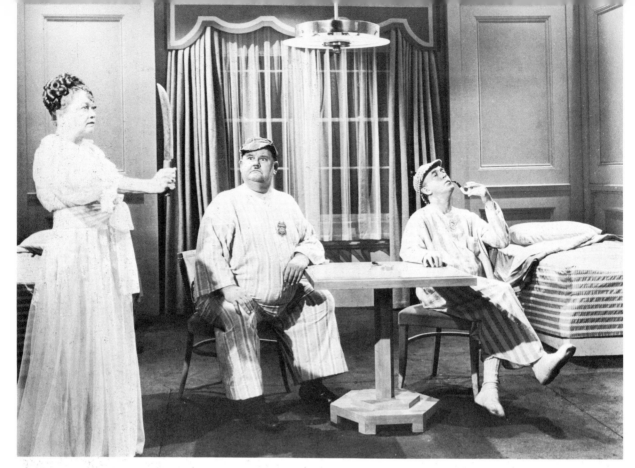

Unlikeliest detectives in The Big Noise.

Admiring the family album (The Big Noise).

aircraft flying through turbulence was brusquely turned down.

The Boys work for a private detective agency, having taken a correspondence course, and are hired by inventor Alva Hartley (Arthur Space) to guard a new explosive device. After surviving the complexities of Hartley's gadget-filled house and his nutty sister-in-law, the Boys fight off villains attempting to steal the invention and somehow manage to capture an enemy submarine. In the course of all this they also survive the perils of being passengers in a remote-controlled aircraft used by the army for target practice.

The Bullfighters (1945) was little better. Once again Mal St Clair directed. He was to make only two more movies, fortunately neither for Laurel and Hardy, before his career ended, in 1948, four years before his death at the age of 55. In the film Stan and Ollie are again private detectives, this time in pursuit of Hattie Blake (Carol Andrews),

Time catching up with The Bullfighters.

149

Unlikely lovebirds: Stan with Margo Woode under Ollie's disapproving eye (The Bullfighters).

Sampling Ollie's cooking in Nothing But Trouble.

whose nickname of Larceny Nell gives a broad hint as to why she is being sought. Trailing her to Mexico, the Boys discover that Stan has a double, none other than Don Sebastian, the famous matador. There follow several unconvincing complications involving rival bullfighter El Brillante (Rory Calhoun) and a confrontation between Stan and a bull.

Hastily put together, and using stock footage from Fox's 1941 re-make of *Blood and Sand*, *The Bullfighters* lacks most qualities motion pictures are supposed to have and Stan and Ollie plainly knew it. From the moment they discovered what working for a big studio really meant, their hearts had not been in any movie they had made. Until these last two films they had managed to conceal the fact from their audiences. Now, they could not hide it; or perhaps they knew there was no longer any point.

For *Nothing But Trouble* (1945) Stan and Ollie are working for a rich family, Stan as the butler and Ollie as chef to the household. Their routine

Nothing But Trouble *looming for two faithful family retainers.*

is interrupted when the exiled young King Christopher of Orlandia (David Leland) comes to stay nearby. The king is in danger from an evil relative, Prince Saul (Philip Merivale), who is planning an assassination. The Boys conceal King Christopher in between cooking such delicacies as horsemeat filched from the lion's cage at the zoo when they are unable to buy steak. After a disastrous dinner party, the Boys are fired. They take the threatened king with them but are assumed to be kidnappers and thrown into jail while Christopher is handed over to the rascally Prince Saul. At Christopher's uging the Boys are released and Saul promptly hires them, planning to use them as scapegoats when he poisons the king at yet another dinner party. After chasing the poison pill through several dishes, Stan and Ollie eventually end up on the ledge of a high window. They are saved from a long fall when Saul finally takes the poison and the king brings the police to the Boys' rescue.

Directed for MGM by Sam Taylor, this film at least has the advantage of looking as if it was made by people who knew some of the business of moviemaking. Sadly, the comedy business was not among their skills and the end result is another dreary affair. Coincidentally, Sam Taylor had also been a writer and director of good-quality comedies in the silent era. He had worked with Harold Lloyd (on *The Freshman* and *The Cat's Paw*), Norma Talmadge, Douglas Fairbanks and Mary Pickford before retiring in 1935. After ten years as a publicist he returned to make just this one film. He should not have bothered.

The heavy hand of the studios, Fox and MGM, was largely responsible for the calamitous decline of Laurel and Hardy in these last films. The absolute and often discourteous refusal of producers, writers and directors to allow them any say in what they were putting on film makes it impossible to attach any blame to Stan and Ollie. Even their increasingly apparent lack of interest in what they were doing is entirely justifiable.

There was another problem, once again not their fault. They had aged. While age did not affect Ollie too adversely (his rotundity remained and helped keep his face comparatively free of wrinkles), Stan was less happily treated by time. Later, when professional and domestic stresses lessened, Stan's appearance improved until serious illness struck.

The ageing process affects more than just the physical appearance of movie stars (and everyone else too). It raises questions of propriety. Everyone has subconscious views on what is acceptable behaviour from people in certain age-groups. Child-like behaviour in the aged or merely ageing causes all manner of psychological problems in the observer. Of course, it also raises problems for the individual himself. For a child-like clown it can be a major psychological blow. In a TV movie made in the 1980s, Dick Van Dyke, a lifelong devotee of Stan Laurel's, stared into his bathroom mirror one morning and said: 'How can I be old when I haven't even grown up yet?' It is a line Oliver Hardy and particularly Stan Laurel might have spoken with feeling at any time in their careers after 1940.

After *Nothing But Trouble* the Boys drifted away from the movies. No one asked them to make another, and after their experiences with both Fox and MGM they had clearly lost interest.

But they wanted to go on working, somehow, somewhere. This turned out to be on the stage again, and in Britain. They left for England in 1947 for a music-hall tour under the auspices of Bernard Delfont. Lucille Hardy went too and so did Stan's new wife, Ida. He had married Ida Kitaeva Raphael in 1946, finding with her the lasting contentment he had failed to discover with his previous wives. Domestically, then, both Stan and Babe were now settled happily and finally. The tour, which lasted nine months and included the London Palladium as well as many provincial cities and towns, used an old favourite of the Boys', their driver's licence sketch.

It was a happy tour. Stan's father, A. J., was still alive and not only he but many of Stan's other relatives were delighted and proud to see this most famous son of the English music hall. The audience response was as adoring as it had been 15 years before and must have diluted the hurt of their recent experiences in Hollywood.

The review of their performance at Hull's New Theatre, printed in that city's *Daily Mail*, was typical, as was the audience response it described: 'They are everything their public hoped for, natural buffoons and as lovable as ever. Children shrieked and adults roared, yet it wasn't the slick wisecrack, just The Thin One and The Fat One, happily awkward. The twiddle of a fat finger and a chubby smile from Oliver, the chalky smile of Stan in his endearing simplicity and the battered bowlers were enough.'

Ollie blowing his bugle for Vera Ralston and John Wayne in The Fighting Kentuckian.

During this engagement, the Boys stayed at the Royal Station Hotel in Hull. One evening, they returned after the show and in the absence of the lift attendant, the floor waiter, Thomas Welburn, took them upstairs. When he recalled the occasion almost 40 years later for Ken Owst, the incident which stuck most firmly in Mr Welburn's mind was that at the first floor, where Stan had a suite, he got out without saying goodnight to Babe (who had a room on the next floor). Perhaps there had been a tough audience that night at the theatre, but it is such moments that might well account for the rumours of dissent which were occasionally appearing in the popular press.

In 1954, Ray Alan felt sufficiently at ease with Babe to ask him about these rumours. They were in Babe's dressing room (which adjoined Stan's, the doors customarily open).

Ray asked him: 'Was it true that at one time you and Stan didn't talk to each other?'

As Ray recalls the occasion, Babe said, 'Yeah,' then gave a little chuckle and called out, 'Hey, Stan!'

'What're you doing, Babe?'

'Come here a minute.' When Stan came into the room, Babe continued. 'Ray's just mentioned when we didn't talk. Do you remember when we read about that in the paper and you said to me, "Hey, look, we're not talking, it says so here in the paper"?'

'Yes, I remember that. Didn't we have a row over something? Wasn't it something to do with my second wife – weren't you going to run away with her?'

'I don't know, something like that.'

'Or didn't I complain that you were on the golf course and never came to rehearse?'

153

Looking for his supper on Atoll K.

'Yeah, I think so. I know we didn't talk to each other though. Certainly it said so in the paper.'

'Yes I remember that.'

And they both smiled quietly.

Before the expiry of Babe's work permit forced them to leave England in 1947, they were invited to appear at the Royal Command Performance before King George VI and Queen Elizabeth. They then took their show to Europe and Scandinavia with a success comparable with that which they had enjoyed in Britain.

When they returned to America it was with much lighter hearts than when they had left. But there was still no film work available for them as a team.

For the first time since making *Zenobia* with Harry Langdon, Oliver Hardy decided to accept a film role without Stan. He made a western, *The Fighting Kentuckian* (1949), which starred John Wayne and Vera Raston. In the role of Willie Payne he provided effective comic relief to Duke's swaggering tough guy. The following year Babe appeared in *Riding High*, a Frank Capra-directed light comedy with a star-studded cast led by Bing Crosby.

Then, unexpectedly, the Boys received an offer to make another film together. Twelve weeks' work in France with a French production company sounded marvellous. Laurel and Hardy were bigger in France than in almost any other country and a movie there surely could not go wrong. In the event, it proved to be a disaster of such thoroughgoing proportions that it was the final film appearance for them both.

In *Atoll K* (1951) the Boys inherit a South Sea island, but on their way there are cast away on an atoll. In company with a young couple (Suzy Delair and Luigi Tosi) they decide to set up a latterday Utopia. (In later desperate attempts to salvage something from the shambles, the film was drastically cut and recut and underwent several title changes, of which *Utopia* was one.) When uranium is discovered on their atoll, all their plans fall apart as criminals descend upon them. Eventually, some measure of peace and tranquillity is restored. On-screen, the performances of Stan and Ollie were as good as circumstances off-screen allowed. Sadly, those off-screen problems were grave.

The production was a mess, and however well-meaning most of the participants might have been no one appeared to have very much idea about making movies. To make matters worse, Stan became seriously ill (which shows dreadfully in his appearance) and was hospitalized for surgery. Though he managed to finish the film, it was not until the original twelve-week schedule had extended to 52 weeks.

Given that Laurel and Hardy had enjoyed careers that were long and gloriously fruitful, it cannot be denied that their reputation today would be just as great had they not made any of their last nine films.

Fortunately for their self-esteem, the Boys were not finished in their roles as entertainers and comedians. There were still more tours of British theatres to make and there was a massive resurgence of interest, popularity and all the former waves of affection and love from audiences old and new when their movies were shown on television. Also yet to come was the rediscovery launched by John McCabe.

Atoll K: *an alternative title for this painful movie is* Utopia, *but it proved to be a far from utopian end to a famous film career.*

James Finlayson with Oliver Hardy.

CHAPTER TEN

On the Loose

The Laurel and Hardy Stock Company

'To Mae Busch – who is eternally ever-popular.'
Toast by the Sons of the Desert

Before moving on to the next stage in the careers of Laurel and Hardy, perhaps it is time to reflect on the players who supported them in many of their classic films. Some were established favourites whose appearance automatically set up expectations of delight in the audience at what was about to happen. With degrees of skill varying from the brilliant to the ordinary they regularly enhanced the Boys' movies and became a valued part of their screen family. The Laurel and Hardy Stock Company, as these actors have been termed, was never strictly that, but certainly the presence on the Hal Roach lot of many dependable if minor acting and comic talents was an important factor in the Boys' successes.

Among the men the best-known was undoubtedly James Henderson Finlayson, known as 'Fin' by all and sundry. He was born in Falkirk, Scotland in the 1880s, where he took his first steps on the stage. He became friendly with Andy Clyde, another Scot who became a mainstay among the supporting actors at the Mack Sennett studios in the 1920s before becoming a regular in the Hopalong Cassidy westerns. In 1911 Fin went to America, where he appeared in New York in the Graham Moffatt play *Bunty Pulls the Strings*, in which he had previously acted in Britain. Taking a liking to America, he worked in vaudeville, touring with Harry Lauder's brother Alec and eventually reaching the West Coast. There he made a number of appearances in movies before joining Mack Sennett in 1920. For Sennett he appeared in *Down on the Farm* (1920), *A Small Town Idol* (1921) and others, but always in roles supporting the likes of Billy Bevan, Ford Sterling

and Ben Turpin. He joined Hal Roach in 1923.

Fin's one-note, high-pressure acting style was restricting. Nevertheless, the demonic mugging, ferocious squint and moustache with a mind of its own (it was false, for Fin was clean-shaven) were all good, if broad, comic material. Playing opposite Stan Laurel and Charley Chase, among many others, he gradually accentuated his eccentric mannerisms until he presented a sharp if unsubtle contrast to their relatively passive personas. In time, his appearance on the cast list of any movie guaranteed that at some point there would be a descent into manic aggression, which marvellously complemented the Boys' ambling ways.

As a member of Hal Roach's All Stars, Fin worked with Laurel and Hardy in the days prior to their official teaming and by the time of his classic appearance in Laurel and Hardy's *Big Business* he had become an important regular. Curiously enough, although the approach of Stan and Ollie was in striking contrast to the frantic Sennett style, Fin carried on the old tradition into the Roach era.

Fin was not exclusively contracted to Roach and also worked for other studios, in particular playing in a series of successful light comedies with another expatriate, actress Dorothy Mackaill, who was born in Hull, England, and became a popular leading lady in Hollywood's low-budget romantic comedies in the late-silent, early-talkie period.

Soon after his enormous success in *Big Business*, the role for which he is rightly best remembered by fans, Fin was faced with the transition to talkies. Just as Laurel and Hardy were blessed

Mae Busch.

with voices that were appropriate to their silent screen personas, so too was Fin. His Scots-accented machine-gun-like delivery was exactly in keeping with his staccato acting style, and as the Boys progressed amiably through the early 1930s Fin was never far away.

Fin made occasional return visits to Britain, making some films and on one occasion accompanying Thelma Todd and Dennis King to the British première of *Fra Diavolo* at the Empire, Leicester Square.

After his 33rd and last appearance with Laurel and Hardy (in *Saps at Sea*), Fin made only a few more films. These included Ernst Lubitsch's brilliant black comedy *To Be Or Not To Be* (1942), which starred Jack Benny, and the Fred Astaire-Jane Powell musical *Royal Wedding* (1951). He died in his sleep in 1953.

If James Finlayson is the best-remembered male member of the Laurel and Hardy supporting company, then Mae Busch is certainly the lady whose name comes first to mind.

Mae was born in 1897 in Melbourne, Australia, where her family was firmly established in the classical music scene. Her mother was an opera singer and her father conductor of the Australian Symphony Orchestra. When she was eight, Mae's family moved to America by way of the South Pacific and she was convent-educated in New Jersey. Entering the movie business, she made her first appearance in *The Agitator* (1912). She divided her early career between film and stage, where she worked with Eddie Foy, one of the Great White Way's most popular entertainers. (Foy would have claimed to be *the* most popular but George Jessell and Al Jolson gave him a run for his money in both popularity and self-esteem.)

Mae was a member of Mack Sennett's famous Bathing Beauties, and was also featured in some Sennett shorts. Her best and most important screen role was in the drama *Foolish Wives* (1922). In this she played opposite Erich Von Stroheim, who also directed. For a while after this Mae did quite well but poor roles, a walk-out and a nervous collapse severely damaged her career until Hal Roach decided that her comic talent could be useful to him.

Mae first appeared with Laurel and Hardy in the pre-teaming *Love 'Em and Weep*, a film in which she was accorded top billing. She also appeared in the Boys' first talkie, *Unaccustomed As We Are*, and soon became a regular interpreter of

Anita Garvin.

the role of a usually malevolent Mrs Hardy. After *The Bohemian Girl* she continued making minor film appearances until her death in 1946 at the age of 49.

Another regular girl in the Laurel and Hardy catalogue seldom makes the pages of even the more comprehensive film encyclopedias. Anita Garvin was an attractive young woman with sparkling green eyes and dramatically black hair who made her stage début in New York, her home town. She became a Ziegfeld girl at the age of 17 before going into the movies in 1925 when she was still only 18.

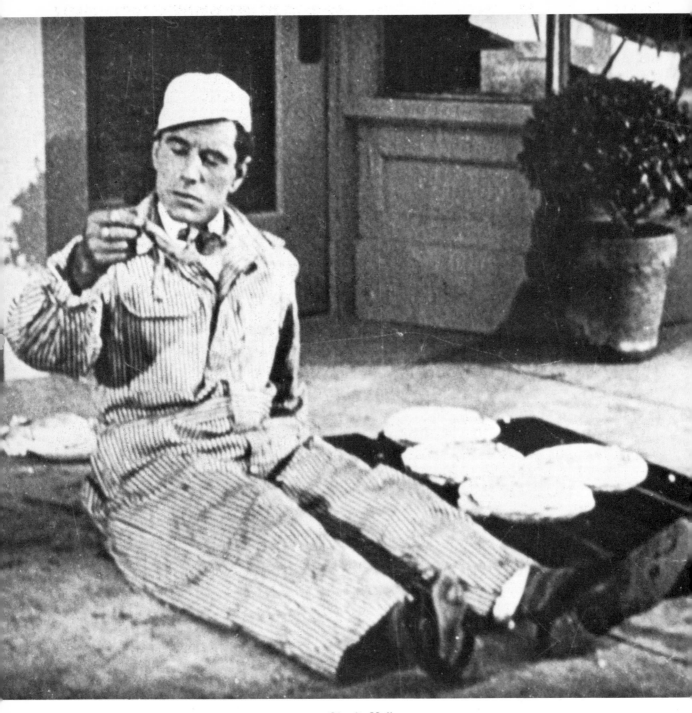

Charlie Hall.

Anita's appearances with Laurel and Hardy began in *With Love and Hisses* and were always effective, as the deft touches she put into her small role in *The Battle of the Century* suggest. She worked in a vast number of films with some of the best actors and moviemakers in the business. She appeared regularly with Charley Chase and towards the end of the 1920s worked in a couple of comedies as co-lead with Marion Byron. This team never had the same impact as Thelma Todd and ZaSu Pitts did in their movies and by the 1930s her career was adrift. She made a brief return from comparative obscurity for a few bit-part appearances with Laurel and Hardy but in the early 1940s returned to obscurity, this time permanently.

Charlie Hall was another regular, making 47 appearances with the Boys. Born in Birmingham,

England, in the 1890s, he moved to America where, although very limited in his acting ability, he proved to be a good foil to Laurel and Hardy and also to Charley Chase. His ability to take punishment with appropriate frustrated anger was perhaps his greatest contribution to Hal Roach's company, together with his reliability and the intangible value of having known faces on the set. He died in 1959.

Baldwin Cooke first met Stan Laurel in vaudeville and he and his wife Alice were the other two-thirds of Stan's act, the Stan Jefferson Trio. Despite the slight hiccup in their working relationship when Stan reformed his group to accommodate his relationship with Mae Dahlberg, the Cookes and Stan remained close friends. Baldy made 30 appearances with the Boys and, as in the case of Charlie Hall, it may well have been his familiarity, allied to the loyalty Stan displayed towards old friends, that most accounted for his regular roles in their movies.

Granite-faced Walter Long occasionally terrorized the Boys. Indeed, Long made a career out of such behaviour, greatly aided by the face of a prizefighter and the build of a wrestler. Blacked up, he played Gus in D. W. Griffith's *The Birth of a Nation* (1915) and he worked in a number of films with Rudolph Valentino. Rychard Cramer was another baddie whose facial expressions instilled fear in Laurel and Hardy on several occasions, most notably as the judge in '*Scram!*' whose wife they inadvertently get drunk. Whenever the Boys needed a comic drunk the role most often went to Arthur Housman, who made a career out of tottering tipsiness (and, according to Stan, managed to imbibe a fair few in real life too).

Harry Bernard, Jack Hill, Sam Lufkin and huge Tiny Sandford (who also worked with Chaplin) between them notched up well over 100 appearances with Laurel and Hardy. There were also occasional roles for stalwarts such as Edgar Kennedy, whose career spanned the early Keystone pictures, Chaplin, Sennett and Roach. His durability and effective use of his trademark, the 'slow burn' response to extreme frustration, eventually earned him his own film series, which ran from 1931 until his death in 1948.

Thelma Todd made a few appearances with the Boys but was best known for her work with Charley Chase and as the co-star in a series with ZaSu Pitts (who was later replaced by Patsy Kelly). When Thelma was asphyxiated in a

Edgar Kennedy.

parked car in 1935 she was only 30 years of age.

Billy Gilbert was another supporting actor whose experience helped lift many more famous players. On the stage from the age of 12 (his parents sang in opera), Billy worked with the Boys in several films, most memorably as the apoplectic Professor Theodore von Schwarzenhoffen in *The Music Box*. He also worked with Chaplin (playing the Hermann Goering figure to Chaplin's

Great Dictator) and was called upon to utilize his famous sneezing routine on the soundtrack of Walt Disney's *Snow White and the Seven Dwarfs* (1938). He worked with the Ritz Brothers, Olsen and Johnson and in the Thelma Todd-ZaSu Pitts comedies. It was Billy Gilbert who one day in vaudeville, when his partner failed to show up for a performance, called on the ticket-seller at the theatre to play his straight man. That was Bud Abbott's entry into show business.

Charley Chase was not a member of the Laurel and Hardy Stock Company though their paths did cross. An extremely able comic with a highly distinctive body language, Chase was an effective actor and director. Among his early screen appearances were several with Chaplin and he worked as director or co-director on films featuring Snub Pollard and Fatty Arbuckle.

As a performer Chase, unlike most of his contemporaries, worked best in sophisticated comedy. In such films he would often appear as a mild-mannered husband with a termagant for a wife. Much of his work can be seen as a forerunner of the domestic sit-com which dominated television from the 1950s onwards. Talkies presented no problems; indeed, his attractive singing voice gave him an edge over his rivals. His important role as the monstrous practical joker in Laurel and Hardy's *Sons of the Desert* added greatly to the success of that movie. As actor and director he made a series of two-reelers, in one of which, *On the Wrong Trek* (1936), Stan and Ollie made a cameo appearance as a pair of (unsuccessful) hitchhikers. Charley Chase (who had guested with Laurel and Hardy and Fin in Max Davidson's *Call of the Cuckoos*) also worked with Andy Clyde and the Three Stooges before his death in 1940 at the age of 46.

Everyone in show business starts somewhere, and if one half of Abbott and Costello began through a chance break with Billy Gilbert, several actors took early, if not their first, steps upward in Laurel and Hardy films.

Jean Harlow is perhaps the most striking example. Working as an extra in films from her mid-teens (and already married), she attracted considerable attention in Laurel and Hardy's *Liberty* and *Double Whoopee* after having the back of her dress ripped off thanks to the Boys' incompetence with a taxicab door. Harlow also appeared in another Roach comedy, *The Unkissed Man*, and was an extra in Chaplin's *City Lights*,

her scenes having been shot before her major breakthrough. This came when, aged 18 and divorced, she was discovered by Howard Hughes and put into *Hell's Angels* (1930). This film was being turned into a talkie, which meant that its foreign leading lady had to be jettisoned. Despite this good start, her career was slow to pick up but her appearance in *The Public Enemy* (1931) with James Cagney helped, as did her move to MGM, where her coarse brassiness was remodelled and she displayed a great flair for comedy.

She was also overtly sexy and after Harlow the blonde in America ceased to be pure and virginal and became the most prominent colouring for sex symbols. Until Marilyn Monroe, no other actress so entranced half of America while simultaneously outraging the other half. Her co-stars included Clark Gable and Spencer Tracy, and for Jean it seemed that the sky was the limit. Her private life was something of a mess, however, but before she had time to capitalize upon her public success or to sort out her personal problems she was taken ill with uraemic poisoning. Shortly afterwards, at only 26, she died from cerebral oedema.

Another actress who came into movies through Hal Roach comedies was Lupe Velez. Her first screen role was in Laurel and Hardy's *Sailors Beware*. She later went on to considerable success in major features, working with such directors as D. W. Griffith and Cecil B. DeMille. In 1934 she was reunited with Laurel and Hardy, the three of them making a brief appearance in a scene in MGM's *Hollywood Party*. Teamed with comic Leon Errol, she made a string of comedy features in her character as the Mexican Spitfire. After several spectacular and public affairs with various men, including Gary Cooper, she married Johnny Weissmuller, then playing Tarzan in the movies, but her battles with him were equally public and divorce soon followed.

Spectacular in life, Lupe Velez was equally spectacular in her death in 1944. Distressed at one desperately unhappy love affair after another and possibly pregnant, she chose to prepare herself with her make-up man and hairdresser before retiring to a flower-decked room in which she took an overdose. She was 36.

Among the male actors who recorded early appearances in Laurel and Hardy films was Robert Blake, who appeared with the Boys in *The Big Noise*. Born in 1933, he began making movies in the late 1930s in the Hal Roach Our Gang shorts. Blake (who was then appearing under his real name of Gubitosi) was one of this ever-changing gang of kids who were extremely popular with audiences of the day. He later turned to supporting roles in westerns but his short stature limited the roles he was offered until the late 1960s, when he began playing leads in major features such as *In Cold Blood* (1968), *Tell Them Willie Boy Is Here* (1969) and *Electra Glide In Blue* (1973). He also became well-known to TV audiences, thanks to his title role in the detective series *Baretta*.

Similarly small in stature was Alan Ladd, who played a bit part in Laurel and Hardy's *Great Guns* which was neither better nor worse than any of the bits he had been playing during the previous decade. The same year as *Great Guns* he was in *Citizen Kane*, with a similar lack of impact. It was not until the following year that Ladd hit the big-time, with roles in *This Gun For Hire* and *The Glass Key*. From then on, despite a minimalist acting technique, he became a box-office hit – although, *Shane* (1953) apart, his films were seldom anything other than well-produced actioners.

Anything but small in stature is Robert Mitchum. When he made *The Dancing Masters* with Laurel and Hardy he was going through the long apprenticeship of bit parts in westerns, gangster movies and dramas which preceded his superstardom. In the 24 months around his one appearance with Laurel and Hardy he made some 25 movies. Only one other of his early films was a comedy. This was *Girl Rush*, which starred RKO's answer to Abbott and Costello, Wally Brown and Alan Carney.

Rory Calhoun appeared in *The Bullfighters* with Stan and Ollie during an apprenticeship which had begun as a result of meeting Alan Ladd. Good-looking in a slightly florid sub-Victor Mature fashion, Calhoun never rose above leads in B-pictures.

However, while these actors were close to the beginnings of careers in which they would enjoy variable degrees of success, Laurel and Hardy were, by the 1950s, close to the end of careers which had touched greatness.

Lupe Velez with the Boys.

In Paris in 1950 (Ida Laurel on left).

CHAPTER ELEVEN

The Finishing Touch
Final Curtains

'It would be unendurable to think that *Atoll K* was the final contribution of Laurel and Hardy to the world of entertainment.'

John McCabe

The experience of making *Atoll K* in France was enough to put anyone off making movies. For a while at least, Stan and Ollie were content not to have to do anything. Not surprisingly, when they had recovered sufficiently from the traumas, they chose the stage for their return to the public eye.

In 1952 they set out for Europe once again, this time for a nine-month tour of British variety theatres. For this, the Boys featured a sketch, 'A Spot of Trouble', written by Stan, which drew some of its inspiration from their film *Night Owls*.

The tour was repeated in 1953-4 and at Cobh, Ireland, an event occurred which Stan later recounted to John McCabe. Often quoted, it bears repetition because it so vividly demonstrates the feeling of their audience towards the Boys, and their response. Thirty-five years since their chance meeting in *Lucky Dog*, and a dozen years since their last decent film, hundreds of people turned out to line the docks. And then the church bells began to ring out their theme song. As Stan recalled, at that moment 'Babe looked at me, and we cried. Maybe people loved us and our pictures because we put so much love in them. I don't know. I'll never forget that day. Never.'

As revealed earlier, the response of Ernie Wise and Eric Morecambe to expressions of the public's affection was a sense of responsibility not to let their audience down. Undoubtedly, Stan and Babe must have been aware that through no fault of their own this was exactly what had happened with their last movies. Now, in personal appearances, they had a chance to make amends.

The 1953-4 show *Birds of a Feather* featured the Boys in a sketch set in a hospital where Ollie is confined following a disastrous attempt to fly like a bird (they played whisky-tasters who had been taking their work too seriously). The sketch was short, a fact which brought their show some fairly offhand reviews in provincial newspapers. Nevertheless, they did attract perceptive attention from Kenneth Tynan, then writing for the London *Daily Sketch*. He mentioned the length of the sketch, about half an hour, summarized it as 'consummately feeble' and recorded that although he did not laugh once, he did smile throughout. What pleased Tynan most was 'the splendid relaxation, the economy of effort with which these two veterans work. They take their time, never forcing the pace; anyone expecting to see a pair of pathetic oldsters straining for laughs will be disappointed.' Tynan ended his review with the comment that Stan and Ollie 'are carrying on a tradition which stretches back to Andrew Aguecheek and Toby Belch. They deserve our respect.'

During the tour the Boys found time for an appearance on BBC Television on 17 October 1953, when they were interviewed on Henry Hall's popular programme *Face the Music*. This tour was also significant for the meeting which took place between Stan and John McCabe. At the time McCabe, an American, was in England as a student at Birmingham University. By chance he learned that Laurel and Hardy were playing at the Birmingham Hippodrome. McCabe went along, enjoyed the show and afterwards, on impulse, went backstage to see if he could meet the Boys for just a moment. The moment extended into many hours and in time McCabe became a close friend of Stan Laurel's. Arising from many meetings, taped interviews and the like came McCabe's first book, *Mr Laurel and Mr Hardy*. This book, which appeared in 1961, together with subsequent titles by McCabe and others, greatly aided the remarkable resurgence of interest in Laurel and Hardy which began during the 1950s.

The audience response to Laurel and Hardy was as enthusiastic as ever and after the recent movie disasters must have proved a great boost for their morale. But there was never any suggestion that they were taking things easy.

Ray Alan, in 1954 a young ventriloquist at an early stage in his career, recalls that neither Stan nor Ollie was prepared to rest on his reputation, nor did they act like the big stars they were:

You have to realize what it was like for me, as an unknown performer, to be working on the bill with them. It was a great thrill, the biggest I've had in show business. Since then I've met members of the Royal Family, but nothing excites me as much as that feeling I had when I first walked into that theatre and there they were. They just smiled and said, 'Hey, you must be Ray. How are you?' I couldn't believe it. It was just beautiful, but then, they were beautiful men.

At Monday morning band call they came into rehearsal like anyone else. Many big stars would have a manager or a musical director who would come in and take the rehearsal but Stan and Babe were always there. And they never wanted to be called Mr Laurel or Mr Hardy; it was always, 'I'm Stan, this is Babe, and that's what you call us.' Their attitude was, we're all working together, we're a team, and it was marvellous. Their doors were always open; if you passed by Babe's door it would be, 'Hiya, Ray, how're you doing?' in his hoarse tones. Because his voice was going a bit towards the end of his life he had to have a microphone. In the sketch that they did, the hospital sketch, he was in a bed and there was a low light hanging over the bed. The microphone was in there.

That sketch was never just left alone. Laurel was always adding to it. When the show finished at night, the last thing on was the sketch. Now normally, at night, the stage hands would strike the set, getting ready for the opening the next day. But, no, that didn't happen with Laurel and Hardy. The set was left up because they came in next morning, got into the set with their hats, stick, whatever props they needed, and were rejigging, improving, pruning, all the time. They were constantly coming up with a new idea. Stan

would say, 'A pause here will get another laugh.' I never heard him say, 'We might get a laugh.' He knew, and that was that.

One of Ray's fondest memories is of when he was leaving the show.

It was at the Newcastle Empire and I was in my dressing room, changing, before going down to watch them and say my goodbyes. There was a knock at the door. I thought it was a stagehand bringing back my music or my front-of-house pictures, but it wasn't. It was Babe Hardy. Now I was upstairs, two-and-a-half flights up, and you have to remember that this man was not well, his legs were bad, and he was big enough to say, 'Ask Ray Alan to come and see me,' and I would've been there like a shot. But no, he'd come up and he had this huge book, like a *Pilgrim's Progress*, and he stood in the doorway and he said, 'Ray, I'm sorry to bother you, but would you mind signing this book. Stan and I, we like to have a record of everybody we work with. Could you sign our book for us?' I couldn't believe it. Here was Babe Hardy asking for *my* autograph and he'd climbed up all these stairs. I glanced very quickly at the book, I saw pictures of a very young Jack Benny, Danny Kaye. Then Babe noticed that I had some little half-postcard photographs, throwaways we used to call them, and he said, 'Oh, and by the way, Ray, do you think you could spare one of these photey-graphs?' I really couldn't believe it.

Babe Hardy's request for Ray Alan's autograph was no exception. During the Boys' engagement at the Palace Theatre in Hull in December 1953 Babe Hardy's infirmity did not prevent him from climbing to the top of the theatre for the chorus girls' signatures in their book. As a young local entertainer, Steve King, observed to Philip Sheard, when the stage manager told Babe he would have sent someone up the stairs on his behalf he was told, 'But Stanley and I wanted the young ladies' autographs . . . *I* was asking the favour, therefore it was up to *me* to approach them.'

From such acts it is clear that the Boys deserved the respect Kenneth Tynan called for on-stage just as much when they were off. In fact, they were on the brink of discovering that there was more than just respect and that the bell-ringing episode at Cobh was no isolated example of how people felt about them.

Within their profession there was no shortage

A tired man: Oliver Hardy in 1950.

of admiration and in England they became members of the Grand Order of Water Rats. Very much taken with the Rats' Jester's Medal offered within the Order for the teller of a really good joke, they suggested a new award. This was the Golden (Wooden) Egg – to be awarded for a really bad one.

Awareness of the extent of public response came when Hal Roach Jr realized that the Boys' old movies were doing excellent business on television. One of them, *Babes in Toyland*, became almost a fixture at Christmas-time. Fan mail, once commonplace but in recent years almost non-existent, began to flood in again.

For Stan and Babe it was a time that must have appeared dreamlike. Their names were on everyone's lips, their work was being applauded and analysed and subjected to far more critical thought than ever it had been in their heyday. Most important to them both, undoubtedly, was the fact that once again the screen capers of Stan and Ollie were making people happy. Unfortunately, Babe's health was failing rapidly.

They were even given the somewhat sickly show-business accolade of a joint appearance on *This Is Your Life*. Ralph Edwards, the show's host, after surprising Stan and Babe in a meeting with Bernard Delfont, was left to ad-lib desperately until the pair made a belated entrance to the studio. It later emerged that Stan, ever insistent upon careful preparation, was reluctant to appear on a show in which his and Babe's contribution was unrehearsed. In the event, once they did walk on to the set, to the customary rapturous applause this show always generates, they were both relaxed and natural and made everyone else look forced and uneasy. Babe's response to an elderly lady who claimed to have been a childhood sweetheart and whom he could obviously barely remember was typically courteous: 'She's still beautiful,' he declared to the sweating Edwards, who was eager to bring on the next guest.

Awkward though some of this show was, television appeared to be where the Boys' future might lie.

A TV series had been suggested and Hal Roach Jr and the Boys got together to work out some ideas. The concept was to be a children's fantasy-land, with many elements familiar to Stan from his knowledge of the old English pantomime. Contracted for four shows, with more if they were successful, it is debatable whether or not they would have been a success. Ernie Wise has expressed some doubts. He and Eric Morecambe entered television from the variety theatres via radio when they were relatively young. In 1955 Stan and Babe were 65 and 63 respectively. The working methods of television anywhere are not easy; the pressures are many. In America in the 1950s it was especially hard and Ernie is probably correct in thinking that the Boys would not have made a successful transition. Ray Alan agrees: 'They were too old, and they no longer had the agility and they hadn't the looks any more. They were old men. On stage it was fine, they had the make-up and everything but after Laurel's illnesses while making *Atoll K* and with Babe's health failing, they looked like two sick elderly gentlemen. They couldn't have coped with all that rehearsal, all those hours in the studio, no fresh air.'

But what if television had been open to them in earlier years? Ray Alan again: 'With them at their peak, they would have moved into TV with no problem at all – Hardy especially, with that camera look. He would have made contact with that one person sitting at home alone. That's what he did when he looked into the lens. He wasn't looking at the camera, he was looking at *you*.'

In the event, speculation is idle for they did not have the chance to try. A little more than a week before the series was to go into production Stan had a stroke.

Stan's illness was mild and he quickly began to pull out of it, but then it was Babe's turn. Suffering from heart trouble, he took medical advice and cut his weight, then over 20 stones, to about 13 stones. Babe's massive weight loss was to no avail and in September 1956 he too suffered a stroke. Unlike his old pal's, this was no mild affair but a massive one which left him without speech and capable of almost no movement.

Seemingly unable to comprehend much of what was going on around him, or, at best, unable to communicate any awareness he might have, Babe's condition deteriorated.

The few visits Stan was able to make when his own ill-health permitted were not happy affairs. Stan was not sure if his words were understood or even if his presence was recognized. In a letter to his friends the Shorts in England he wrote, 'Poor fellow is in bad shape and still confined to bed . . . it's certainly distressing.'

A newspaper report suggests that Babe was

Dining out in style.

aware of the depths of his plight and that on one occasion, still unable to speak, he managed to write on a pad the words: 'Anything's better than this.'

The illness dragged on until 7 August 1957, when Babe died at the home of Lucille Hardy's mother in North Hollywood. He was 65.

'What's there to say?' the press reported Stan as saying. 'It's shocking, of course. Ollie was like a brother. That's the end of the history of Laurel and Hardy.'

Stan was forbidden by his doctor to attend the funeral, but Ida Laurel was there to comfort Lucille and among the mourners were Hal Roach and Andy Clyde.

In the sense in which Stan meant it, the history of Laurel and Hardy *was* over, but in the wider sense nothing could have been further from the truth. In the years following Oliver Hardy's death the resurgence of interest in and enthusiasm for the Boys' work continued to grow. Their movies were shown on television in most countries of the world.

In recognition of the interest shown in the Boys John McCabe, Al Kilgore and others helped establish a permanent tribute with the formation of the Sons of the Desert in New York. A buff club rather than a fan club, the Sons of the Desert, now numbering many thousands worldwide (all grouped in 'tents', as the individual chapters are called), meet, talk about Laurel and Hardy, screen films, maintain contact with one another, with actors from the old films and with relatives and friends of Stan and Babe. Stan helped formulate the articles of the association's constitution, which established, among many less-than-serious regulations, one major principle: that the Sons of the Desert is an organization which has 'scholarly overtones and heavily social undertones devoted to the loving study of the persons and films of Stan Laurel and Oliver Hardy'.

Thanks to the books about the Boys, interest continued to swell through the early 1960s and Stan received countless letters from fans the world over. Assiduously, he attempted to answer every letter personally from his home at the Oceana Apartment Hotel, Santa Monica. In particular, he corresponded with his fans in England, a country for which he never lost his affection. Indeed, he always remained a British citizen.

In 1961 he was awarded a special Oscar for 'creative pioneering in the field of cinema comedy'. As Laurel was unable to attend through ill-health, the award was accepted on his behalf by Danny Kaye.

Stan's health varied but for the most part he had managed to thrust off the effects of the mild stroke that had immediately preceded Babe's final illness. He travelled a little, managing a holiday in Italy in 1964, watched television endlessly, often offering to interested companions such as John McCabe pithy comments upon the work of latter-day comics. And he visibly relished visits from comedians he admired, like Dick Van Dyke, and who so obviously admired him.

In February 1965 Stan, now 74, suffered a heart attack and was confined to bed. Ida cared for him as the final act in a marriage which had, miraculously, confounded all expectations by being long and loving. But she also needed professional help and it was a nurse who was with him on 23 February when Stan cracked his final gag. As his biographers reported it, Stan addressed the nurse: 'I'd rather be skiing than doing this.' 'Do you ski, Mr Laurel?' the innocent lady enquired. 'No,' said Stan, 'but I'd rather be doing that than this.'

With perfect comic timing, the next moment he was dead.

CHAPTER TWELVE

Leave 'Em Laughing

Happy Memories

'That line, you should quote it somewhere in your
book: "two funny, gentle men".'

Ray Alan

The history of popular culture is well scattered
with examples of public taste coming into conflict
with prevailing critical opinion. Given endless
opportunity for revision of their previously expressed views, critics can and regularly do change
their minds. Public opinion does not enjoy such
opportunities for correcting itself when it gets
things wrong but can take consolation in quiet
crowing when the critics later come round to the
same way of thinking.

In the case of Laurel and Hardy some critics,
especially in America, damned them with faint
praise while heaping Chaplin and Keaton with
intellectual accolades they had never sought and
could not justify. In Keaton's case the burden was
not responsible for the crippling of his career;
with Chaplin the effect was damaging because his
was a personality that accepted intellectual
worship as nothing more than his due.

Laurel and Hardy were spared the often dead
hand of critical acclaim in their lifetimes and to a
great extent have not had to endure it since. If it
were to happen now, it probably would not matter
much, although it would be sad to think of their
movies being pored over and dissected instead of
simply being enjoyed. Their place, either way, is
secure.

Sadly, the continuing legal problems surround-
ing the Boys' work, arguments over exactly who
owns the copyright to many of their short films,
and even their names and images, began while
Stan was still alive and dragged on into the 1980s.
None of this can have helped their widows. (Ida
Laurel died in 1980, Lucille Hardy Price in 1986.)
Were they able to do so, doubtless Stan and Babe

would regard such activities in wonderment –
possibly tinged with a touch of resignation that
despite the staggering technical advances of the
past decade or so, the motion-picture industry is
still at heart a petty small town. Almost certainly
the Boys would not feel bitter, although they
would have every right to do so. Fortunately for
their numerous fans, by 1987 most of the problems appeared to have been resolved.

The arguments were essentially about money,
which is ironic in the light of the Boys' personal
financial straits. Though rumours of their living in
abject poverty were unfounded, for neither was
poor during his lifetime and their dependants
were similarly comfortable, their monetary re-
wards were not remotely commensurate with the
millions of dollars their work has generated.

Whatever Laurel and Hardy's financial legacy
may have been, their comic legacy is another
matter. Entertainers of their day and shortly
thereafter knowingly benefited and were always
eager to acknowledge their debt. Today the direct
influence may be less obvious. Many younger
entertainers may be using ideas and methods
created by the Boys without acknowledgement,
simply because they are unaware of the source. If
they are modelling their style on someone who,
years ago, modelled *his* style on Stan or Ollie,
then the connection becomes understandably
tenuous. Closely modelled on Stan is a character
regularly seen on British television screens. When
Ray Alan was seeking a suitably inebriated face
for a new doll for his ventriloquist's act, he could
not get it quite right. Then he noticed an auto-
graphed picture of the Boys he keeps on his office

wall. There was the expression he wanted: Stan Laurel's – eyelids already slightly down, maybe a touch less vague, smoothed-down hair and a monocle. That became Lord Charles, so now, everywhere that Ray goes, he carries a little reminder of Laurel and Hardy in his suitcase.

There have also been attempts to recreate their qualities on stage. In the winter of 1976-7 the Tom McGrath play *Mr Laurel and Mr Hardy* ran at London's Mayfair Theatre. With John Shedden as Stan Laurel and Ian Ireland as Oliver Hardy, the play traced their life story. It met with only limited success. Another, slightly more successful, play was *Blockheads*, written by Michael Landwehr, Kay Cole and Arthur Whitelaw. Produced at the Mermaid Theatre in London in 1984, this play starred British actor Mark Hadfield as Laurel and American Kenneth H. Waller as Hardy, aided by Simon Browne as Fin and Larry Dann, who played several other major characters in the Boys' lives. Like its predecessor this piece attempted to summarize the Boys' careers. In 1985 the musical *Stan and Ollie*, by Ron Day and Nicky Paule, played to some success in the north of England. All these stage presentations achieved most of their objectives but, perhaps inevitably, gave little indication of the source of all that warmth and affection which suffuses Laurel and Hardy's work and which are the principal factors keeping their spirit alive today.

That spirit is maintained in part by the Sons of the Desert in their myriad tents throughout America and Britain and in other countries including France, Holland and Japan. It is maintained by the affectionate tributes written by John McCabe and others; and by the tiny memorabilia-filled Laurel and Hardy museum run by Bill Cubin in Stan's home town of Ulverston (now in Cumbria).

But most of all the spirit is maintained by the Boys themselves, whether on 8mm film screened in the homes of their fans, or on 16mm and 35mm films used at Laurel and Hardy festivals, or on television, or in the new computer-enhanced 'colorized' video films produced in America – to a reception in which technical hype clashed head-on with worried doubts from the faithful who prefer the original monochrome.

Colorization and its rival Color Systems Technology are computer processes by which black and white movies are coloured using as a guideline any predetermined information that may exist – colour of eyes, hair, clothing, and so on – together with advice given by an art director. When a computer-coloured print of the film is combined with a normal monochrome version of the film the original gradations in colour (caused by light and shade) create an impressive effect.

Among the studios actively interested in and encouraging this development is Hal Roach's and, as reported in the October 1986 issue of *TV World*, high on its list of priorities are several Laurel and Hardy films. Three Colorized films were complete: *Way Out West*, *Helpmates* and *The Music Box*. If the early Colorized films were of doubtful quality, *Way Out West* showed a marked improvement, and with *The Music Box* an astonishingly high standard had been reached. Of course, there are some who doubt the validity of colouring a film that was made in monochrome. As Hal Roach (who is no longer connected with the studio that bears his name) commented in 1986: 'Yes, but does it make them any funnier?'

Perhaps more important to the long-term view of Stan and Ollie is the likelihood of Colorization widening the appeal of the films to younger audiences whose experience of film and television is such that they think a film is somehow lacking in quality simply because it is in black and white.

An equally notable development is that the Hal Roach Studios have begun restoring many of the monochrome films using new techniques to remove scratches and by late 1986 had a total of 26 90-minute compilations ready for release. These include previously unissued clips – outtakes from Laurel and Hardy's films. Such new items, together with those rediscovered foreign-language versions, to say nothing of such rumoured discoveries as the long-lost *Why Girls Love Sailors* (1927), will keep their legend alive.

In whatever form Laurel and Hardy appear to fans and to newcomers to their work, it is less their entire body of work that explains what makes them so special than a moment here, a scene there, an image, a word or just a look. At the time of Babe's death an article in *The New York Times* reflected: 'There was a genuine craftsmen's lack of pretension about Laurel and Hardy movies. They weren't masterpieces; you rarely recall their names, and never the situations, juvenile leads or pretty actresses intermixed with the comic episodes. You recall only skinny Laurel playing against fat Hardy as a bow plays against a fiddle, and you think of the gay, ingenious music.'

To suggest that none of their films is a masterpiece is only one man's opinion – against which many would argue furiously – but there is none the less an element of truth in this comment.

The little bits of comic business that illuminate even their lesser works are recalled with unending delight. Selecting some of those marvellous moments is inevitably an exercise in idiosyncrasy, as is choosing favourite paintings, music, food or wines. What one will choose another might reject, and, indeed, anyone compiling such a list might well find disagreement himself the next time because of a change in mood or circumstance. Yet every fan does it, whether a Son of the Desert, a casual observer with happy memories of times past or a youngster coming to the Boys' work for the first time.

Apart from the presence of Stan and Ollie, all such chosen moments have something in common: a guarantee that they will generate laughter. They might include the long-delayed last brick that falls down the chimney to hit Ollie on the head in *Dirty Work*, or the last, thunderous fall off the roof in *Hog Wild*; the sustained build-up of the sequence of gags in *Perfect Day* which surrounds Edgar Kennedy's bandaged foot; the wholesale destruction of cars in the closing moments of *Two Tars*; the studied expertise of the culminating pie-throwing scene in *The Battle of the Century* and the orgy of personal violence in the pants-pulling, shin-kicking scene in *You're Darn Tootin'*; the inevitability of the destruction of Ollie's home in *Helpmates*; Stan and Ollie's giggling helplessness in *'Scram!'*; almost every moment of *Big Business* and every foot of the laborious-yet-glorious struggle up the steps in *The Music Box*.

And, of course, there are the countless camera looks from Ollie at Stan's hopeless incompetence; and the moments when Stan, hands clasped loosely behind him, studies with wondrous detachment the chaos he has created.

These and many, many more are the jewels in the crown of Stan Laurel and Oliver Hardy's golden career. It is a career which can never be repeated. As the distinguished critic James Agee remarked, 'We will never see their like again.'

Truly, we will not: the conditions which gave them their unmatched qualities no longer exist. Gone are the traditions of the English music hall and the silent comedy factories of early Hollywood. There are now and will continue to be other double-acts, but they will be different because their training grounds have changed.

As time passes and the reasons for laughter in our present-day world become increasingly rare, the contribution to popular culture of Stan Laurel and Oliver Hardy becomes steadily more valuable.

In their careers they earned respect, admiration, affection and love and proved that, contrary to the daily headlines, the human race is not so bad after all.

For that, and for all the laughter they gave so generously, they deserve our unreserved and unlimited gratitude.

Filmography

Extensive and painstaking research by Richard W. Bann has produced the definitive filmography of Laurel and Hardy up to 1975. Readers who require full details of all films are directed to his work (see McCabe, Kilgore and Bann in the Bibliography). Here, with the assistance of Glenn Mitchell, I have sought to update Bann's work with newly discovered information, although there remains scope for more research as archives continue to yield long-buried treasure.

This listing includes all known films in which Stan Laurel and Oliver Hardy both appear.

All films comprise two reels, are silent and black and white unless otherwise stated.

Between 1926 and 1939 (inclusive) unless otherwise stated the production company is Hal Roach Productions and the producer is Hal E. Roach.

Precise release dates have not been stated as not all can be verified.

Abbreviations
PC Production company; *P* Producer; *D* Director; *Sc* Screenplay; *Sv* Supervisor; *Ph* Photographer; *C* Cast (Laurel and Hardy are not listed every time). *AS*: All Star Series; *LHS*: Laurel and Hardy Series; MGM: Metro-Goldwyn-Mayer; TCF: Twentieth Century-Fox.

Where a film title is followed by * this indicates that at least one foreign-language version was made; in some cases these were longer or edited together into features.

The company name appearing in brackets after each film title is the releasing company.

1917

Lucky Dog P: Gilbert M. Anderson. *D:* Jess Robbins. *C:* Florence Gillet.

1921

The Rent Collector Joint appearance of Laurel and Hardy still unconfirmed (see text).

1926

45 Minutes from Hollywood (Pathé) *D:* Fred L. Guiol. *Sc:* Hal Roach. *C:* Glen Tryon, Charlotte Mineau, Rube Clifford, Sue O'Neil (Molly O'Day), Theda Bara, Edna Murphy, Jerry Mandy, Ham Kinsey, Ed Brandenberg, Jack Hill, Al Hallet, Tiny Sandford, Our Gang (Mickey Daniels, Scooter Lowry, Allen Hoskins, Jackie Condon, Jay R. Smith, Johnny Downs, Joe Cobb), the Hal Roach Bathing Beauties.

1927

Duck Soup (Pathé) *AS* (based on story by A. J. Jefferson). *D:* Fred L. Guiol. *C:* Madeleine Hurlock, William Austin, Bob Kortman.

Slipping Wives (Pathé) *AS D:* Fred L. Guiol. *Sc:* Hal Roach. *Sv:* F. Richard Jones. *Ph:* George Stevens. *C:* Priscilla Dean, Herbert Rawlinson, Albert Conti.

Love 'Em and Weep (Pathé) *AS D:* Fred L. Guiol. *Sc:* Hal Roach. *C:* Mae Busch, James Finlayson,

Charlotte Mineau, Vivien Oakland, Charlie Hall, May Wallace, Ed Brandenberg, Gale Henry.

Why Girls Love Sailors (Pathé) *AS D*: Fred L. Guiol. *Sc*: Hal Roach. *C*: Viola Richard, Anita Garvin, Malcolm Waite.

With Love and Hisses (Pathé) *AS D*: Fred L. Guiol, *Sc*: Hal Roach. *C*: James Finlayson, Frank Brownlee, Chet Brandenberg, Anita Garvin, Eve Southern, Will Stanton, Jerry Mandy, Frank Saputo, Josephine Dunn.

Sugar Daddies (MGM) *AS D*: Fred L. Guiol. *Ph*: George Stevens. *C*: James Finlayson, Noah Young, Charlotte Mineau, Edna Marian, Eugene Pallette, Charlie Hall, Jack Hill, Sam Lufkin, Dorothy Coburn, Ray Cooke.

Sailors, Beware (Pathé) *AS D*: Hal Yates. *Sc*: Hal Roach. *C*: Anita Garvin, Tiny Sandford, Viola Richard, May Wallace, Connie Evans, Barbara Pierce, Lupe Velez, Will Stanton, Ed Brandenberg, Dorothy Coburn, Frank Brownlee, Harry Earles, Charley Young.

The Second Hundred Years (MGM) *AS D*: Fred L. Guiol. *C*: James Finlayson, Eugene Pallette, Tiny Sandford, Ellinor Van Der Veer, Charles A. Bachman, Edgar Dearing, Otto Fries, Bob O'Conor, Frank Brownlee, Dorothy Coburn, Charlie Hall, Rosemary Theby.

Call of the Cuckoos (MGM) (Max Davidson Series) *D*: Clyde A. Bruckman. *Sv*: Leo McCarey. *Ph*: Floyd Jackman, *C*: Max Davidson, Lillian Elliott, Spec O'Donnell, Charley Chase, James Finlayson, Frank Brownlee, Charlie Hall, Charles Meakin, Leo Willis, Lyle Tayo, Edgar Dearing, Fay Holderness, Otto Fries.

Hats Off (MGM) *AS D*: Hal Yates. *Sv*: Leo McCarey. *C*: James Finlayson, Anita Garvin, Dorothy Coburn, Ham Kinsey, Sam Lufkin, Chet Brandenberg. (No copy known to exist.)

Do Detectives Think? (Pathé) *AS D*: Fred L. Guiol. *Sc*: Hal Roach. *C*: James Finlayson, Viola Richard, Noah Young, Frank Brownlee, Will Stanton, Charley Young, Charles A. Bachman.

Putting Pants on Philip (MGM) *AS D*: Clyde A.

Bruckman, *Ph*: George Stevens. *C*: Sam Lufkin, Harvey Clark, Ed Brandenberg, Dorothy Coburn, Chet Brandenberg, Retta Palmer, Bob O'Conor, Eric Mack, Jack Hill, Don Bailey, Alfred Fisher, Lee Phelps, Charles A. Bachman.

The Battle of the Century (MGM) *AS D*: Clyde A. Bruckman. *Sc*: Hal Roach. *Sv*: Leo Mc Carey. *Ph*: George Stevens. *C*: Dick Gilbert, George K. French, Sam Lufkin, Noah Young, Gene Morgan, Al Hallet, Anita Garvin, Eugene Pallette, Lyle Tayo, Charlie Hall, Dorothy Coburn, Ham Kinsey, Bert Roach, Jack Hill, Bob O'Conor, Ed Brandenberg, Dorothy Walbert, Charley Young, Ellinor Van Der Veer, crowd extra: Lou Costello. (Pie fight and boxing scenes survive, remainder presently unavailable.)

1928

Leave 'Em Laughing (MGM) *AS D*: Clyde A. Bruckman. *Sc*: Hal Roach. *Sv*: Leo McCarey. *Ph*: George Stevens. *C*: Edgar Kennedy, Charlie Hall, Viola Richard, Dorothy Coburn, Tiny Sandford, Sam Lufkin, Edgar Dearing, Al Hallet, Jack V. Lloyd, Otto Fries, Jack Hill.

Flying Elephants (Pathé) *AS D*: Fred Butler. *Sc*: Hal Roach. *C*: Dorothy Coburn, Leo Willis, Tiny Sandford, Bud Fine.

The Finishing Touch (MGM) *AS D*: Clyde A. Bruckman. *Sv*: Leo McCarey. *Ph*: George Stevens. *C*: Edgar Kennedy, Dorothy Coburn, Sam Lufkin.

From Soup to Nuts (MGM) *AS D*: Edgar Kennedy. *Sc*: Leo McCarey. *Sv*: Leo McCarey. *Ph*: Len Powers. *C*: Anita Garvin, Tiny Sandford, Otto Fries, Edna Marian, Ellinor Van Der Veer, George Bichel, Dorothy Coburn, Sam Lufkin, Gene Morgan.

You're Darn Tootin' (UK title: *The Music Blasters*) (MGM) *AS D*: Edgar Kennedy. *Sv*: Leo McCarey. *Ph*: Floyd Jackman. *C*: Sam Lufkin, Chet Brandenberg, Christian Frank, Rolfe Sedan, George Rowe, Agnes Steele, Ham Kinsey, William Irving, Charlie Hall, Otto Lederer, Dick Gilbert, Frank Saputo.

Their Purple Moment (MGM) *AS D*: James Parrott. *Sv*: Leo McCarey. *Ph*: George Stevens. *C*: Anita Garvin, Kay Deslys, Jimmy Aubrey, Fay Holderness, Lyle Tayo, Leo Willis, Jack Hill, Retta Palmer, Tiny Sandford, Sam Lufkin, Ed Brandenberg, Patsy O'Byrne, Dorothy Walbert.

Should Married Men Go Home? (MGM) *LHS D*: James Parrott. *Sc*: Leo McCarey and James Parrott. *Sv*: Leo McCarey. *Ph*: George Stevens. *C*: Edgar Kennedy, Edna Marian, Viola Richard, John Aassen, Jack Hill, Dorothy Coburn, Lyle Tayo, Chet Brandenberg, Sam Lufkin, Charlie Hall, Kay Deslys.

Early to Bed (MGM) *LHS D*: Emmett Flynn. *Sv*: Leo McCarey. *Ph*: George Stevens. *C*: Laurel and Hardy alone (plus dog 'Buster').

Two Tars (MGM) *LHS D*: James Parrott. *Sc*: Leo McCarey. *Sv*: Leo McCarey. *Ph*: George Stevens. *C*: Thelma Hill, Ruby Blaine, Charley Rogers, Edgar Kennedy, Clara Guiol, Jack Hill, Charlie Hall, Edgar Dearing, Harry Bernard, Sam Lufkin, Baldwin Cooke, Charles McMurphy, Ham Kinsey, Lyle Tayo, Lon Poff, Retta Palmer, George Rowe, Chet Brandenberg, Fred Holmes, Dorothy Walbert, Frank Ellis, Helen Gilmore. (A contemporary trade advertisement reads: 'with sound', suggesting music and effects.)

Habeas Corpus (MGM) *LHS D*: Leo McCarey. *Sc*: Leo McCarey. *Sv*: Leo McCarey. *Ph*: Len Powers. *C*: Richard Carle, Charles A. Bachman, Charley Rogers. (Released with music and effects.)

We Faw Down (MGM) *LHS D*: Leo McCarey. *C*: George Kotsonaros, Bess Flowers, Vivien Oakland, Kay Deslys, Vera White, Allen Cavan. (Released with music and effects.)

1929

Liberty (MGM) *LHS D*: Leo McCarey. *Sc*: Leo McCarey. *Ph*: George Stevens. *C*: James Finlayson, Tom Kennedy, Jean Harlow, Harry Bernard, Ed Brandenberg, Sam Lufkin, Jack Raymond, Jack Hill. (Released with music and effects.)

Wrong Again (MGM) *LHS D*: Leo McCarey. *Sc*: Leo McCarey, Lewis R. Foster. *Ph*: George Stevens, Jack Roach. *C*: Del Henderson, Harry

Bernard, Charlie Hall, William Gillespie, Jack Hill, Sam Lufkin, Josephine Crowell, Fred Holmes. (Released with music and effects.)

That's My Wife (MGM) *LHS D*: Lloyd French. *Sc*: Leo McCarey. *Sv*: Leo McCarey. *C*: Vivien Oakland, Charlie Hall, Jimmy Aubrey, William Courtwright, Sam Lufkin, Harry Bernard. (Released with music and effects.)

Big Business (MGM) *LHS D*: James W. Horne. *Sc*: Leo McCarey. *Sv*: Leo McCarey. *Ph*: George Stevens. *C*: James Finlayson, Tiny Sandford, Lyle Tayo, Retta Palmer, Charlie Hall.

From this point onwards, all films are talkies unless stated otherwise.

Unaccustomed As We Are (MGM) *LHS D*: Lewis R. Foster. *Sc*: Leo McCarey. *C*: Mae Busch, Thelma Todd, Edgar Kennedy. (Until late 1970s available only in silent version.)

Double Whoopee (MGM) *LHS* Silent. *D*: Lewis R. Foster. *Sc*: Leo McCarey. *Ph*: George Stevens, Jack Roach. *C*: Tiny Sandford, Charlie Hall, Jean Harlow, Rolfe Sedan, Sam Lufkin, William Gillespie, Charley Rogers, Ed Brandenberg.

*Berth Marks** (MGM) *LHS D*: Lewis R. Foster. *Sc*: Leo McCarey. *Ph*: Len Powers. *C*: Harry Bernard, Baldwin Cooke, Charlie Hall, Pat Harmon, Silas D. Wilcox; reputed extra: Paulette Goddard.

Men o'War (sometimes erroneously reissued as *Man o'War*) (MGM) *LHS D*: Lewis R. Foster. *Ph*: George Stevens, Jack Roach. *C*: James Finlayson, Harry Bernard, Anne Cornwall, Gloria Greer, Pete Gordon, Charlie Hall, Baldwin Cooke.

Perfect Day (MGM) *LHS D*: James Parrott. *Sc*: Hal Roach, Leo McCarey. *C*: Edgar Kennedy, Kay Deslys, Isabelle Keith, Harry Bernard, Clara Guiol, Baldwin Cooke, Lyle Tayo, Charley Rogers, dog 'Buddy'.

They Go Boom (MGM) *LHS D*: James Parrott. *Sc*: Leo McCarey. *C*: Charlie Hall, Sam Lufkin.

Bacon Grabbers (MGM) *LHS* Silent but released with music and effects. *D*: Lewis R. Foster. *Sc*: Leo McCarey. *Ph*: George Stevens. *C*: Edgar Kennedy, Jean Harlow, Charlie Hall, Bobby Dunn, Eddie Baker, Harry Bernard, Sam Lufkin.

The Hoose-Gow (MGM) *LHS D*: James Parrott. *Sc*: Leo McCarey. *Ph*: George Stevens, Len Powers, Glenn Robert Kershner. *C*: James Finlayson, Tiny Sandford, Leo Willis, Dick Sutherland, Ellinor Van Der Veer, Retta Palmer, Sam Lufkin, Eddie Dunn, Baldwin Cooke, Jack Ward, Ham Kinsey, John Whiteford, Ed Brandenberg, Chet Brandenberg, Charles Dorety, Charlie Hall.

The Hollywood Revue of 1929 PC: MGM. *P*: Harry Rapf. *D*: Charles F. Reisner. *Sc*: Al Boasberg, Robert E. Hopkins and others. *Ph*: Maximilian Fabian and others. *C*: Jack Benny, Conrad Nagel, Joan Crawford, Marion Davies, Buster Keaton, Norma Shearer, John Gilbert, Lionel Barrymore, Ann Dvorak, Bessie Love, Marie Dressler, Cliff Edwards and others, Some sequences of this revue film are in Technicolor. Laurel and Hardy in one sketch. Running time: 115 minutes.

Angora Love (MGM) *LHS*: Silent with music and effects. *D*: Lewis R. Foster. *Sc*: Leo McCarey. *Ph*: George Stevens. *C*: Edgar Kennedy, Charlie Hall, Harry Bernard, Charley Young.

1930

*Night Owls** (MGM) *LHS D*: James Parrott. *Sc*: Leo McCarey. *Ph*: George Stevens. *C*: Edgar Kennedy, James Finlayson, Anders Randolph, Harry Bernard, Charles McMurphy, Baldwin Cooke.

*Blotto** (MGM) *LHS D*: James Parrott. *Sc*: Leo McCarey. *Ph*: George Stevens. *C*: Anita Garvin, Tiny Sandford, Baldwin Cooke, Charlie Hall, Frank Holliday, Dick Gilbert, Jack Hill. (3 reels; most British copies cut to 2, however.)

*Brats** (MGM) *LHS D*: James Parrott. *Sc*: Leo McCarey, Hal Roach. *Ph*: George Stevens. *C*: Laurel and Hardy alone, each in dual roles.

*Below Zero** (MGM) *LHS D*: James Parrott. *Sc*: Leo McCarey. *Ph*: George Stevens. *C*: Charlie Hall, Frank Holliday, Leo Willis, Tiny Sandford, Kay Deslys, Blanche Payson, Lyle Tayo, Retta Palmer, Baldwin Cooke, Bobby Burns, Jack Hill.

The Rogue Song PC: MGM. Technicolor. *P-D*: Lionel Barrymore (Laurel and Hardy directed by Hal Roach). *Sc*: Frances Marion, John Colton. *Ph*: Percy Hilburn, C. Edgar Schoenbaum. *C*: Lawrence Tibbett, Catherine Dale Owen, Judith Voselli, Nance O'Neil, Florence Lake, Lionel Belmore, Ulrich Haupt, Kate Price, Wallace McDonald, Burr McIntosh, James Bradbury, H.A. Morgan, Elsa Alsen, Harry Bernard. (Lost film: a few minutes with Laurel and Hardy was discovered in 1981. Entire soundtrack, on disc, discovered c.1980.)

Hog Wild (UK title: *Aerial Antics*)* (MGM) *LHS D*: James Parrott. *Sc*: Leo McCarey. *Ph*: George Stevens. *C*: Fay Holderness, Dorothy Granger, Charles McMurphy.

*The Laurel and Hardy Murder Case** (MGM) *LHS D*: James Parrott. *Ph*: George Stevens, Walter Lundin. *C*: Tiny Sandford, Fred Kelsey, Bobby Burns, Del Henderson, Dorothy Granger, Frank Austin, Lon Poff, Rosa Gore, Stanley Blystone, Art Rowlands. 3 reels.

*Another Fine Mess** (MGM) *LHS D*: James Parrott. *Sc*: H. M. Walker from a story by A. J. Jefferson. *Ph*: George Stevens. *C*: Thelma Todd, James Finlayson, Eddie Dunn, Charles Gerrard, Gertrude Sutton, Harry Bernard, Bill Knight, Bob Mimford, Bobby Burns, Joe Mole. 3 reels.

1931

*Be Big** (MGM) *LHS D*: James Parrott. *Sc*: H. M. Walker. *Ph*: Art Lloyd. *C*: Anita Garvin, Isabelle Keith, Charlie Hall, Baldwin Cooke, Jack Hill, Ham Kinsey, Chet Brandenberg. 3 reels.

*Chickens Come Home** (MGM) *LHS D*: James W. Horne. *Sc*: H. M. Walker. *Ph*: Art Lloyd, Jack Stevens. *C*: Mae Busch, Thelma Todd, James Finlayson, Frank Holliday, Elizabeth Forrester, Norma Drew, Patsy O'Byrne, Charles French, Gertrude Pedlar, Frank Rice, Gordon Douglas, Ham Kinsey, Baldwin Cooke, Dorothy Layton. 3 reels. (Sometimes entitled *Chicken Come Home* in reissues.)

The Stolen Jools (UK title: *The Slippery Pearls*) (Paramount/National Screen Services) *PC*: National Variety Artists (fund-raising film) *P*: Pat Casey. *D*: William McGann. *C*: Wallace Beery, Buster Keaton, Edward G. Robinson, Our Gang, Norma Shearer, Hedda Hopper, Joan Crawford, Victor McLaglen, Wheeler and Woolsey, Gary Cooper, Maurice Chevalier, Loretta Young, Bebe Daniels, Ben Lyon, Fay Wray and many others. (Discovered early 1970s.)

*Laughing Gravy** (MGM) *LHS D*: James W. Horne. *Sc*: H. M. Walker. *Ph*: Art Lloyd. *C*: Charlie Hall, Harry Bernard, Charles Dorety, dog 'Laughing Gravy'. (Rejected sequence recently discovered.)

*Our Wife** (MGM) *LHS D*: James W. Horne. *Sc*: H. M. Walker. *Ph*: Art Lloyd, *C*: Jean 'Babe' London, James Finlayson, Ben Turpin, Charley Rogers, Blanche Payson.

Pardon Us (UK title: *Jailbirds*)* (MGM) *D*: James Parrott. *Sc*: H. M. Walker. *Ph*: Jack Stevens. *C*: Walter Long, James Finlayson, June Marlowe, Charlie Hall, Sam Lufkin, Harry Bernard, Tiny Sandford, Bobby Burns, Wilfred Lucas; bits: James Parrott, Hal Roach and others.

Come Clean (MGM) *LHS D*: James W. Horne. *Sc*: H. M. Walker. *Ph*: Art Lloyd. *C*: Gertrude Astor, Linda Loredo, Mae Busch, Charlie Hall, Eddie Baker, Tiny Sandford, Gordon Douglas.

One Good Turn (MGM) *LHS D*: James W. Horne. *Sc*: H. M. Walker. *Ph*: Art Lloyd. *C*: Mary Carr, James Finlayson, Billy Gilbert, Lyle Tayo, Dorothy Granger, Snub Pollard, Gordon Douglas, Dick Gilbert, Baldwin Cooke, George Miller, Ham Kinsey, Retta Palmer, Charley Young, William Gillespie.

Beau Hunks (UK title: *Beau Chumps*) (MGM) *LHS D*: James W. Horne. *Sc*: H. M. Walker. *Ph*: Art Lloyd, Jack Stevens. *C*: Charles Middleton, Charlie Hall, Tiny Sandford, Harry Schultz, Gordon Douglas, Sam Lufkin, Marvin Hatley, Jack Hill, Leo Willis, Bob Kortman, Baldwin Cooke, Dick Gilbert, Oscar Morgan, Ham Kinsey, Broderick O'Farrell, James W. Horne (as 'Abdul Kasin K'Horne'). 4 reels.

On the Loose (MGM) (Pitts-Todd Series) *D*: Hal Roach. *Sc*: H. M. Walker, Hal Roach. *Ph*: Len Powers. *C*: Thelma Todd, ZaSu Pitts, Claud Allister, John Loder, Billy Gilbert, Charlie Hall, Gordon Douglas, Jack Hill, Buddy MacDonald, Otto Fries. (Laurel and Hardy make only a cameo appearance.)

1932

Helpmates (MGM) *LHS D*: James Parrott. *Sc*: H. M. Walker. *Ph*: Art Lloyd. *C*: Blanche Payson, Bobby Burns, Robert Callahan.

Any Old Port (MGM) *LHS D*: James W. Horne. *Sc*: H. M. Walker. *Ph*: Art Lloyd. *C*: Walter Long, Julie Bishop (as Jacqueline Wells), Harry Bernard, Charlie Hall, Bobby Burns, Sam Lufkin, Dick Gilbert, Eddie Baker, Will Stanton, Jack Hill, Baldwin Cooke, Ed Brandenberg. Cut from 3 reels prior to release.

The Music Box (MGM) *LHS D*: James Parrott. *Sc*: H. M. Walker. *Ph*: Walter Lundin, Len Powers. *C*: Billy Gilbert, William Gillespie, Charlie Hall, Gladys Gale, Sam Lufkin, Lilyan Irene. 3 reels.

The Chimp (MGM) *LHS D*: James Parrott. *Sc*: H. M. Walker. *Ph*: Walter Lundin. *C*: Billy Gilbert, James Finlayson, Tiny Sandford, Charles Gamora, Jack Hill, Bobby Burns, George Miller, Baldwin Cooke, Dorothy Layton, Belle Hare, Martha Sleeper. 3 reels.

County Hospital (MGM) *LHS D*: James Parrott. *Sc*: H. M. Walker. *Ph*: Art Lloyd. *C*: Billy Gilbert, Sam Lufkin, Baldwin Cooke, Ham Kinsey, May Wallace, Frank Holliday, Lilyan Irene, Belle Hare, Dorothy Layton, William Austin. 3 reels.

'Scram!' (MGM) *LHS D*: Raymond McCarey. *Sc*: H. M. Walker. *Ph*: Art Lloyd. *C*: Arthur Housman, Rychard Cramer, Vivien Oakland, Sam Lufkin, Charles McMurphy, Baldwin Cooke, Charles Dorety. 3 reels.

Pack Up Your Troubles D: George Marshall (Ray McCarey also credited but seemingly in error). *Sc*: H. M. Walker. *Ph*: Art Lloyd. *C*: Tom Kennedy, Grady Sutton, Donald Dillaway, Jacqui Lyn, Mary Carr, Billy Gilbert, C. Montague Shaw, Muriel Evans, James Finlayson, Frank Brownlee,

Charley Rogers, Jack Hill, Ham Kinsey, Charlie Hall, Rychard Cramer, Dick Gilbert. 7 reels.

Their First Mistake (MGM) *LHS D*: George Marshall. *C*: Mae Busch, Billy Gilbert, George Marshall.

Towed in a Hole (MGM) *LHS D*: George Marshall. *Ph*: Art Lloyd. *C*: Billy Gilbert.

1933

Twice Two (MGM) *LHS D*: James Parrott. *Ph*: Art Lloyd. *C*: Laurel and Hardy in dual roles, Baldwin Cooke, Charlie Hall, Ham Kinsey.

Me and My Pal (MGM) *LSH D*: Charles Rogers, Lloyd French. *Ph*: Art Lloyd. *C*: James Finlayson, James C. Morton, Eddie Dunn, Charlie Hall, Bobby Dunn, Carroll Borland, Mary Kornman, Charles McMurphy, Eddie Baker, Marion Bardell, Charley Young, 'Walter Plinge'.

Fra Diavolo (MGM) *D*: Hal Roach, Charles Rogers. *Sc*: Jeanie MacPherson. *Ph*: Art Lloyd, Hap Depew. *Music*: Daniel F. Auber. *C*: Dennis King, Thelma Todd, James Finlayson, Henry Armetta, Lane Chandler, Arthur Pierson, Tiny Sandford, John Qualen, Harry Bernard. 9 reels.

The Midnight Patrol (MGM) *LHS D*: Lloyd French. *Ph*: Art Lloyd. *C*: Robert Kortman, Charlie Hall, 'Walter Plinge', Harry Bernard, Frank Brownlee, James C. Morton, Tiny Sandford, Edgar Dearing, Eddie Dunn, Billy Bletcher.

Busy Bodies (MGM) *LHS D*: Lloyd French. *Ph*: Art Lloyd. *C*: Tiny Sandford, Charlie Hall, Jack Hill, Dick Gilbert, Charley Young.

Wild Poses (MGM) (Our Gang Series) *P-D*: Robert F. McGowan. *Ph*: Francis Corby. *C*: Spanky McFarland, Stymie Beard, Tommy Bond, Darby Billings, Jerry Tucker, Franklin Pangborn, Emerson Treacy, Gay Seabrook. (Laurel and Hardy appear in cameo roles.)

Dirty Work (MGM) *LHS D*: Lloyd French. *Ph*: Kenneth Peach. *C*: Lucien Littlefield, Sam Adams.

Sons of the Desert (UK title: *Fraternally Yours*)

(MGM) *D*: William A. Seiter. *Sc*: Frank Craven. *Ph*: Kenneth Peach. *C*: Charley Chase, Mae Busch, Dorothy Christy, Lucien Littlefield, Charley Young, John Elliott, Harry Bernard, Baldwin Cooke, Sam Lufkin. 7 reels.

1934

Oliver the Eighth (MGM) *LHS D*: Lloyd French. *Ph*: Art Lloyd. *C*: Mae Busch, Jack Barty. 3 reels.

Hollywood Party PC: MGM. *P*: Harry Rapf, Howard Dietz. *D*: Richard Boleslawski, Allan Dwan. *Sc*: Howard Dietz, Arthur Kober. *Ph*: James Wong Howe. *C*: Jimmy Durante, Lupe Velez, The Three Stooges, Ted Healy, Frances Williams, Robert Young, Eddie Quillan, Jack Pearl. (Laurel and Hardy in lengthy guest appearance.) Disney sequences in Technicolor.

Going Bye-Bye! (MGM) *LHS D*: Charles Rogers. *Ph*: Francis Corby. *C*: Walter Long, Mae Busch, Sam Lufkin, Harry Dunkinson, Ellinor Van Der Veer, Baldwin Cooke, Tiny Sandford, Lester Dorr, Charles Dorety, Fred Holmes.

Them Thar Hills (MGM) *LHS D*: Charles Rogers. *Ph*: Art Lloyd. *C*: Billy Gilbert, Charlie Hall, Mae Busch, Bobby Dunn, Sam Lufkin, Dick Alexander, Eddie Baker, Baldwin Cooke, Bobby Burns.

Babes in Toyland (MGM) *LHS D*: Charles Rogers, Gus Meins. *Sc*: Nick Grinde, Frank Butler. *Ph*: Art Lloyd, Francis Corby. *Music*: Victor Herbert. *C*: Charlotte Henry, Felix Knight, Henry Brandon, Johnny Downs, Jean Darling, Marie Wilson, Virginia Karns, Florence Roberts, William Burress, Ferdinand Munier. 9 reels. (Reissued variously as *March of the Wooden Soldiers, March of the Toys, Toyland,* etc.)

The Live Ghost (MGM) *LHS D*: Charles Rogers. *Ph*: Art Lloyd. *C*: Walter Long, Mae Busch, Arthur Housman, Harry Bernard, Charlie Hall, Sam Lufkin, Baldwin Cooke, Les Willis.

1935

Tit For Tat (MGM) *LHS D*: Charles Rogers. *Ph*: Art Lloyd. *C*: Charlie Hall, Mae Busch, James C. Morton, Bobby Dunn, Baldwin Cooke, Jack Hill.

The Fixer Uppers (MGM) *LHS D*: Charles Rogers. *Ph*: Art Lloyd. *C*: Mae Busch, Charles Middleton, Arthur Housman, Bobby Dunn, Noah Young.

Thicker Than Water (MGM) *LHS D*: James W. Horne. *Sc*: Stan Laurel. *Ph*: Art Lloyd. *C*: Daphne Pollard, James Finlayson, Harley Bowen, Ed Brandenberg, Charlie Hall, Grace Goodall, Bess Flowers, Lester Dorr, Gladys Gale, Allen Cavan, Baldwin Cooke.

Bonnie Scotland (MGM) *D*: James W. Horne. *Sc*: Frank Butler, Jefferson Moffitt. *Ph*: Art Lloyd, Walter Lundin, *C*: Anne Grey, David Torrence, June Lang, William Janney, James Mack, James Finlayson, Mary Gordon, May Beatty, Daphne Pollard, James May, Jack Hill, Marvin Hatley. 8 reels.

1936

The Bohemian Girl (MGM) *D*: James W. Horne, Charles Rogers. *Ph*: Art Lloyd, Francis Corby. *Music*: Michael W. Balfe. *C*: Julie Bishop (as Jacqueline Wells), James Finlayson, Mae Busch, Antonio Moreno, William P. Carlton, Harry Bernard, Sam Lufkin, Felix Knight, Thelma Todd, dog 'Laughing Gravy'. 7 reels.

On the Wrong Trek (MGM) (Charley Chase series) *D*: Charles Parrott (Charley Chase), Harold Law. *Ph*: Art Lloyd. *C*: Charley Chase, Rosina Lawrence, Bonita Weber, Charles McAvoy, Bob O'Conor and others. Laurel and Hardy in a cameo appearance.

Our Relations (MGM) *P*: Stan Laurel. *D*: Harry Lachman. *Sc*: Richard Connell, Felix Adler. *Ph*: Rudolph Maté. *C*: Laurel and Hardy in dual roles, Sidney Toler, Alan Hale, Daphne Pollard, Betty Healy, Iris Adrian, Lona Andre, James Finlayson, Arthur Housman, Charlie Hall, Harry Bernard, Baldwin Cooke, Tiny Sandford. 7 reels.

1937

Way Out West (MGM) *P*: Stan Laurel. *D*: James W. Horne. *Sc*: Charles Rogers, Felix Adler, James Parrott. *Ph*: Art Lloyd, Walter Lundin. *C*: James Finlayson, Sharon Lynne, Rosina Lawrence, Vivien Oakland, Stanley Fields, Harry Bernard, Sam Lufkin, Jack Hill, the Avalon Boys Quartet (inc. Chill Wills). 6 reels.

Pick a Star (MGM) *D*: Edward Sedgwick. *Sc*: Richard Flournoy, Arthur Vernon Jones, Thomas J. Dugan. *Ph*: Norbert Brodine, Art Lloyd. *C*: Patsy Kelly, Rosina Lawrence, Jack Haley, Mischa Auer, Lyda Roberti, James Finlayson, Walter Long. (Laurel and Hardy appear in two sequences.) 8 reels.

1938

Swiss Miss (MGM) *D*: John G. Blystone. *Sc*: James Parrott, Felix Adler, Charles Melson. *Ph*: Norbert Brodine, Art Lloyd. *C*: Walter Woolf King, Della Lind, Anita Garvin, Eric Blore, Charles Judels, Charles Gamora, Ludovico Tomarchio, Adia Kuznetzoff. 7 reels.

Block-Heads (MGM) *D*: John G. Blystone. *Sc*: Charles Rogers, Felix Adler, James Parrott, Harry Langdon, Arnold Belgard. *Ph*: Art Lloyd. *C*: Billy Gilbert, Patricia Ellis, Minna Gombell, James C. Morton, James Finlayson, Harry Woods, Sam Lufkin. 5 reels.

1939

The Flying Deuces PC: RKO. *P*: Boris Morros. *D*: A. Edward Sutherland. *Sc*: Ralph Spence, Alfred Schiller, Charles Rogers, Harry Langdon. *Ph*: Art Lloyd. *C*: Jean Parker, Reginald Gardner, James Finlayson, Charles Middleton, Rychard Cramer. 7 reels (often cut in UK copies).

1940

A Chump at Oxford (United Artists) *D*: Alfred Goulding. *Sc*: Charles Rogers, Felix Adler, Harry Langdon. *Ph*: Art Lloyd. *C*: Forrester Harvey, Wilfred Lucas, James Finlayson, Anita Garvin, Harry Bernard, Peter Cushing, Charlie Hall. US: 4 reels; Europe: 6 reels.

Saps at Sea (MGM) *D*: Gordon Douglas. *Sc*: Charles Rogers, Felix Adler, Gil Pratt, Harry Langdon. *Ph*: Art Lloyd. *C*: James Finlayson, Ben Turpin, Rychard Cramer, Charlie Hall, Jack Hill, Harry Bernard, Sam Lufkin. 6 reels.

1941

Great Guns PC: TCF. *P*: Sol M. Wurtzel. *D*: Monty Banks. *Sc*: Lou Breslow. *Ph*: Glen Mac-

Williams. *C*: Mae Marsh, Ethel Griffies, Sheila Ryan, Dick Nelson, Edmund MacDonald, Kane Richmond. 74 minutes.

1942

A-Haunting We Will Go PC: TCF. *P*: Sol M. Wurtzel. *D*: Alfred Werker. *Sc*: Lou Breslow. *Ph*: Glen MacWilliams. *C*: Harry A. Jansen, Sheila Ryan, John Shelton, Don Costello, Elisha Cook Jr, Ed Gargan, Mantan Moreland, Willie Best, Diana Rochelle (Margaret Roach, daughter of Hal). 67 minutes.

1943

The Tree in a Test Tube (Kodachrome color, 16mm) *PC* US Defense Dept. *D*: Charles Mac-Donald. *Ph*: A. H. C. Sintzenich. *C*: Laurel and Hardy alone (silent with voice-over by Pete Smith). 1 reel.

Air Raid Wardens PC: MGM. *P*: B. F. Zeidman. *D*: Edward Sedgwick. *Sc*: Martin Rackin, Jack Jevne, Charles Rogers, Harry Crane. *Ph*: Walter Lundin. *C*: Edgar Kennedy, Jacqueline White, Stephen McNally, Russell Hicks, Nella Walker, Howard Freeman, Donald Meek. 67 minutes.

Jitterbugs PC: TCF. *P*: Sol M. Wurtzel. *D*: Malcolm St Clair. *Sc*: Scott Darling. *Ph*: Lucien Andriot. *C*: Vivian Blaine, Robert Bailey, Lee Patrick, Francis Ford, Douglas Fowley. 74 minutes.

The Dancing Masters PC: TCF. *P*: Lee Marcus. *D*: Malcolm St Clair. *Sc*: Scott Darling. *Ph*: Norbert Brodine. *C*: Trudy Marshall, Robert Bailey, Matt Briggs, Margaret Dumont, Allan Lane, Daphne Pollard, Robert Mitchum. 63 minutes.

1944

The Big Noise PC: TCF. *P*: Sol M. Wurtzel. *D*: Malcolm St Clair. *Sc*: Scott Darling. *Ph*: Joe MacDonald. *C*: Jack Norton, Veda Ann Borg, Doris Merrick. Arthur Space, Robert Blake. 74 minutes.

1945

The Bullfighters PC: TCF. *P*: William Girard. *D*:

Malcolm St Clair. *Sc*: Scott Darling. *Ph*: Norbert Brodine. *C*: Margo Woode, Richard Lane, Carol Andrews, Rory Calhoun, Diosa Costello, Ralph Sanford. 69 minutes.

Nothing But Trouble PC: MGM. *P*: B. F. Ziedman. *D*: Sam Taylor. *Sc*: Russell Rouse, Ray Golden. *Ph*: Charles Salerno Jr. *C*: Henry O'Neill, Mary Boland, David Leland, Matthew Boulton, Philip Merivale. 70 minutes.

1951

Atoll K PC: Les Films Sirius, Franco-London Films, Fortezza Films. *P*: Raymond Eger, Paul Joly. *D*: Leo Joannon, John Berry, Alf Goulding. *Ph*: Armand Thiraro, Louis Nee. *C*: Suzy Delair, Max Elloy, Suzet Mais, Felix Oudart. 9 reels, often shortened. Also released as *Utopia, Robinson Crusoe-Land*, etc.

Selected Laurel and Hardy Compilations

The Golden Age of Comedy (1958), *When Comedy Was King* (1960), *Days of Thrills and Laughter* (1961), *Thirty Years of Fun* (1964), *M-G-M's Big Parade of Fun* (1964), *Laurel and Hardy's Laughing Twenties* (1965) (all foregoing compiled and produced by Robert Youngson), *The Crazy World of Laurel and Hardy* (Jay Ward, 1965), *The Further Perils of Laurel and Hardy* (Robert Youngson, 1967), *Four Clowns* (Robert Youngson, 1970), *The Best of Laurel and Hardy* (James L. Wolcott, 1971).

Various home movies have come to light, including a studio gag reel entitled *That's That!* assembled for Stan Laurel, and some between-takes shots. Others include film of their 1932 visits to Tynemouth and Edinburgh, a post-war item taken with Stan's cousin Nancy Wardell, and colour footage of the team on-stage in America during a wartime tour. The Pathé News library includes many items from the 1947 to 1953 visits to UK. British Movietone News' coverage of their 1947 trip on the Romney, Hythe and Dymchurch Railway is the most frequently seen news film. A 1950 interview exists of Oliver Hardy talking about his career and the forthcoming *Atoll K*.

There have also been some compilations on television which have included Laurel and Hardy sequences.

The following broadcast details were supplied to the Sons of the Desert by the BBC. The initial enquiry was in connection with a film interview conducted by Eamonn Andrews shown on television in the 1970s and not re-shown since.

Radio

26 July 1932	National	4-minute interview
29 May 1947	North	Dressing-room interview on *Morecambe Night Out*
23 October 1953	Midland	Interview by Philip Garston-Jones on *What Goes On*

Television

20 February 1952	Interview by Leslie Mitchell on *Picture Page*
17 October 1953	Comedy interview scripted by Sid Colin and Talbot Rothwell on *Face the Music*
18 April 1961	Film of Stan Laurel in Africa on *Tonight*

One notable TV documentary was *Cuckoo* (shown in 1974 in BBC TV's *Omnibus* series), a profile of the team with interviews, stills and clips, introduced by Eric Morecambe and Ernie Wise.

Radio documentaries include *Mr Laurel and Mr Hardy* (BBC Radio 4, 1975), written by Michael Pointon and presented by Roy Castle; *I Call It Genius: Laurel & Hardy* (BBC Radio 2, 1980), written and presented by Hubert Gregg.

In the early 1960s W. T. Rabe compiled a radio documentary including on-stage recordings, interviews, clips and narration: this project, which was later adapted for use by Voice of America, remains a major work on the team.

One American broadcast which can be enjoyed today is the 1938 pilot show *The Wedding Party*, with Edgar Kennedy and Patsy Moran in support. The text is available in John McCabe's *The Comedy World of Stan Laurel* while the recording itself may be heard on the LP *Laurel and Hardy on the Air* (q.v.).

Laurel and Hardy in Britain

(courtesy of the *Laurel and Hardy Magazine*)

Laurel and Hardy toured Britain and Europe during 1932, 1947-8, 1952 and 1953-4. Full details are presently unavailable but the last UK tours were as follows:

1952 tour

25 February-8 March
Embassy, Peterborough

10-15 March
Empire, Glasgow

17 March
Empire, Newcastle

24 March
Empire, Sunderland

31 March
Royal, Hanley

7 April
Empire, Leeds

14 April
Empire, Nottingham

21 April
Granada, Shrewsbury

28 April
Empire, Edinburgh

5 May
Hippodrome, Birmingham

12 May
Gaumont, Southampton

19 May
Empire, Liverpool

26 May-7 June
Olympia, Dublin, Eire

9-21 June
Grand Opera House, Belfast

30 June
Empire, Sheffield

7 July
Hippodrome, Brighton

14 July
Palace, Manchester

21 July
Queens, Rhyl

28 July
Alhambra, Bradford

4 August
Odeon, Southend-on-Sea

11 August
Hippodrome, Coventry

18 August
Garrick, Southport

25 August
Granada, Sutton

1 September
Hippodrome, Bristol

8 September
Theatre Royal, Portsmouth

15 September
Hippodrome, Dudley

22 September
Empire, Swansea

29 September
New, Cardiff

1953-4 tour

19 October
New, Northampton

26 October
Empire, Liverpool

2 November
Hippodrome, Manchester

9 November
Empire, Finsbury Park (cancelled due to Stan's illness)

16 November
Empress, Brixton

23 November
Empire, Newcastle

30 November
Hippodrome, Birmingham

7 December
Palace, Hull

21 December-16 January
Empire, Nottingham

18 January
Theatre Royal, Portsmouth

25 January
Empire, Chiswick

1 February
Empire, Finsbury Park

8 February
Hippodrome, Brighton

15 February
Hippodrome, Norwich

22 February
Empire, Sunderland

1 March
Empire, Glasgow

8 March
Hippodrome, Wolverhampton

15 March
Empire, Sheffield

22 March
Empire, York

29 March
Palace, Grimsby

5 April
Empire, Leeds

12 April
Empire, Edinburgh

19 April
Her Majesty's, Carlisle

3 May
Alhambra, Bradford

10 May
Hippodrome, Aston

17 May
Palace, Plymouth (curtailed following Oliver Hardy's illness)

Select Discography

LPs featuring excerpts from films

Naturally High
Douglas 10

The Golden Age of Hollywood Comedy: Laurel and Hardy
United Artists UAG 29676

Another Fine Mess
United Artists UAG 30010

Laurel and Hardy
Mark 56 575

Another Fine Mess
Mark 56 579

In Trouble Again!
Mark 56 600

No U-Turn
Mark 56 601

A Nostalgia Trip to the Stars Vol. 2
Monmouth-Evergreen MES 7031

The Movie Collection
Deja Vu DVLP 2054

Film Star Parade
ASV Living Era 5020

Soundtrack albums

Babes in Toyland
Mark 56 577

Sons of the Desert
Mark 56 689

The Rogue Song
Pelican LP 2019

Miscellaneous material

Voices from the Hollywood Past (interview with Stan)
Delos DEL F25412

Laurel and Hardy on the Air
Radiola MR 1104

The Golden Age of Comedy
Charisma PCS 11

78 rpm records

Voice of the Stars (excerpt from *Sons of the Desert*)
Regal-Zonophone MR 1234

Hal Roach and MGM present Laurel and Hardy (sketch and music recorded in London 1932) (N.B. This material appears in whole or in part on the LPs from Charisma, Radiola, Monmouth-Evergreen, ASV Living Era.)
Columbia DX 370

45 rpm records

'The Trail of the Lonesome Pine' with the Avalon Boys, Chill Wills, Rosina Lawrence from *Way Out West*/'Honolulu Baby' with Ty Parris and Charley Chase from *Sons of the Desert* (US version: Mark 56 303)
United Artists UP 36026

'Another Fine Mess' (with the Boston Barbers)/'The Stan and Ollie Serenade' with the Boston Serenaders (soundtrack clips linked with music)
United Artists UP 36107

'You Are the Ideal of My Dreams' from *Beau Hunks*/'Let Me Call You Sweetheart' from *Swiss Miss*
United Artists UP 36164

'Shine on, Harvest Moon' from *The Flying Deuces*/'The World Is Waiting for the Sunrise' from *The Flying Deuces*.
Columbia DB 9145

Bibliography

Agee, James, *Agee on Film* (London: Owen, 1963)

Barr, Charles, *Laurel & Hardy* (London: Studio Vista, 1967)

Bier, Jesse, *The Rise and Fall of American Humor* (New York: Hippocrene, 1980)

Brownlow, Kevin, *Hollywood: the Pioneers* (London: Collins, 1979)

Chaplin, Charles, *My Autobiography* (London: Penguin Books, 1966)

Chester, Charlie, *The Grand Order of Water Rats* (London: W.H. Allen, 1984)

Dardis, Tom, *Keaton: the Man Who Wouldn't Lie Down* (London: André Deutsch, 1979)

Durgnat, Raymond, *The Crazy Mirror: Hollywood Comedy and the American Image* (London: Faber and Faber, 1969)

Everson, William K., *The Films of Laurel and Hardy* (Secaucus: Citadel, 1967)

Gallagher, J.P., *Fred Karno: Master of Mirth and Tears* (London: Hale, 1971)

Guiles, Fred Lawrence, *Stan* (London: Michael Joseph, 1980)

Hardy, Forsyth, ed., *Grierson on the Movies* (London: Faber and Faber, 1981)

Katz, Ephraim, *The International Film Encyclopedia* (London: Macmillan, 1979)

Kerr, Walter, *The Silent Clowns* (New York: Knopf, 1975)

Koszarski, Richard, *Hollywood Directors 1914-1940* (New York: OUP, 1976)

Lahue, Kalton C., *World of Laughter* (Norman Okla.: University of Oklahoma Press, 1972)

McCabe, John, *Charlie Chaplin* (London: Magnum, 1979)

McCabe, John, *The Comedy World of Stan Laurel* (London: Robson, 1975)

McCabe, John, Kilgore, Al, and Bann, Richard W., *Laurel & Hardy* (London: W.H. Allen, 1975)

McCabe, John, *Mr Laurel and Mr Hardy* (London: Robson, 1976)

Maltin, Leonard, *The Great Movie Shorts* (New York: Bonanza, 1972)

Maltin, Leonard, ed., *The Laurel & Hardy Book* (New York: Curtis, 1973)

Maltin, Leonard, *Movie Comedy Teams* (New York: NAL, 1970)

Mast, Gerald, *The Comic Mind* (London: NEL, 1974)

Mellor, G.J., *The Northern Music Hall* (Newcastle: Frank Graham, 1970)

Owen-Pawson, Jenny and Mouland, Bill, *Laurel Before Hardy* (Kendal: Westmorland Gazette, 1984)

Rosenberg, Bernard and Silverstein, Harry, *The Real Tinsel* (London: Macmillan, 1970)

Scagnetti, Jack, *The Laurel and Hardy Scrapbook* (New York: Jonathan David, 1976)

Sheard, Philip, 'Laurel and Hardy Visit Any Old Port' in *Bowler Dessert* no.23, August 1986

Sobel, Raoul and Francis, David, *Chaplin: Genesis of a Clown* (London: Quartet, 1977)

Welford, Ross, 'Take it as Red. . .' in *TV World*, October 1986.

Other magazine and newspaper articles referred to are acknowledged in the text.

Acknowledgements

I wish to express my sincere gratitude to Glenn Mitchell, who read my work, corrected several errors of fact, and who directed my thoughts in interesting and productive ways. Without his efforts those parts of this book which deal with early film history and in particular the film career of Laurel and Hardy would be much less than they are now. Needless to say, should any errors of fact remain undetected in this book they are my responsibility.

Anyone writing today on Laurel and Hardy owes an inestimable debt to the pioneering work of Professor John McCabe. His books are invaluable and warmly recommended.

In addition I wish to acknowledge the help of many others: some offered suggestions, screened films for me, read an early draft typescript, offered opinions and comments (although the opinions expressed are mine), or simply talked about Stan and Ollie for my benefit. To all of them, named below or not, I wish to express my sincere thanks.

Ray Alan, who talked long and fascinatingly of his tour with Laurel and Hardy; Tony Barker, of *Music Hall* magazine for the loan of material; Roy Castle, who shared with me his opinions of their work; Dave Dalton, who screened many long-forgotten films from his vast collection; Robert S. Lewis, who pointed me towards all the right people; Ken Owst, who allowed me to share the results of his researches; Philip Sheard, who also showed me films and loaned me articles and memorabilia; Carol Tuck, for her Laurel and Hardy 'masks' illustration; Dave Tuck, who read, criticized and offered advice, and, alphabetically last but by no means least, Ernie Wise, who gave me his invaluable insight into the workings of comedy duos.

B.C.

Picture Credits

Some of the illustrations in this book come from stills issued to publicize films made or distributed by the following companies: Hal Roach Productions, Franco-London Films, MGM, Twentieth Century-Fox.

Pictures are reproduced courtesy of Richard W. Bann and the British Film Institute.

Although efforts have been made to trace the present copyright holders of all photographs, the publishers apologize in advance for any unintentional omission or neglect and will be pleased to insert the appropriate acknowledgement to companies or individuals in subsequent editions of this book.

Index

Page numbers in bold type refer to illustrations.

Abbott, Bud, 135, 162
Abbot and Costello, 39, 117, 135, 136, 140, 162, 163
Adrian, Iris, 105
Age, d'or, L', 56
Agee, James, 37, 175
Agitator, The, 159
A-Haunting We Will Go, 140, **141**
Air Raid Wardens, **140**, 141, 144
Alan, Ray, 10, 12, 133, 134, 153, 166, 168, 171
Anderson, Gilbert M., 17, 19, 21
Andre, Lona, 105
Andrews, Carole, 149
Angora Love, 60, **61**, 77
Another Fine Mess, **73**, 75
Any Old Port, 84
Arbuckle, Roscoe 'Fatty', 123, 124, 127, 162
Ardell, Alyce, 101
Astaire, Fred, 159
Atoll K, **154**, 155, **155**, 165, 168
Aubrey, Jimmy, 19

Babes in Toyland, 96, **97**, **98**, 168
Babe's School Days, 19
Bacon Grabbers, 54, 59
Bailey, Robert, 144, 146
Balfe, Michael, 102
Bann, Richard W., 19, 68
Baretta (TV), 163
Barnes, Peter, 102, 133
Battle of the Century, The, 43, 135, 146, 160, 175
Battling Butler, 126
Beau Hunks, 82, **83**
Be Big, 69, **75**, 77
Beery, Wallace, 78
Below Zero, 69, **69**
Bennett, Constance, 115
Benny, Jack, 159
Bernard, Harry, 54, 161
Berth Marks, **62**, 63, 147
Best, Willie, 140
Bevan, Billy, 157
Bier, Jesse, 134
Big Business, 56, **58**, 59, 157, 175
Big House, The, 78
Big Noise, The, 147, **148**, 163
Birds of a Feather (stage), 165
Birth of a Nation, The, 161
Blaine, Vivian, 144
Blake, Robert, 162, 163
Blockheads (stage), 174
Block-Heads, 108, **110**, 111
Blood and Sand (1922), 19
Blood and Sand (1941), 150
Blotto, 68, 69
Bohemian Girl, The, 102, **103**, **104**, 159

Bonnie Scotland, **100**, 102
Brandon, Henry, **97**
Brats, **68**, 69
Brown, Wally, 136, 163
Browne, Simon, 174
Bruckman, Clyde, 39, 45, 124, 126, 135
Buck Privates, 140
Bullfighters, The, 149, **149**, 150, **150**, 163
Buñuel, Luis, 56
Bunty Pulls the Strings (stage), 157
Burns, Bobby, **84**
Busch, Mae, 41, 63, 77, **90**, 94, **95**, 99, 102, 127, 157, **158**, 159
Busy Bodies, **94**
Byron, Marion, 160

Cagney, James, 162
Calhoun, Rory, 150, 163
Call of the Cuckoos, 44, **44**, 162
Capra, Frank, 130, 154
Carney, Alan, 136, 163
Carr, Mary, 82
Castle, Roy, 122, 135
Cat's Paw, The, 130, 152
Chaplin, Charles Sr, 121
Chaplin, Charlie, 9, 10, 12, 13, **13**, 16, 17, 19, 29, 30, 35, 60, 102, 118, **120**, 121-3, 124, 126, 128, 130, 131, 133, 161, 162, 171
Chase, Charley, 19, 20, 23, **42**, 51, **95**, 157, 160, 161, 162
Chickens Come Home, 69, 77
Chien andalou, Un, 56
Chimp, The, **88**
Christy, Dorothy, 94
Chump at Oxford, A, **116**, 117
Circus, The, 123
Citizen Kane, 163
City Lights, 123, 162
Clyde, Andy, 157, 162, 170
Cole, Kay, 174
College, 126, 127
Come Clean, **81**
Comedy World of Stan Laurel, The (McCabe), 9
Comic, The, 136
Conkin, Chester, 121
Coogan, Jackie, 126
Cooke, Alice, 17, 161
Cooke, Baldwin, 17, 161
Cooper, Gary, 162
Corbett, James J., 19
Costello, Lou, 135
County Hospital, 85, 88
Cramer, Rychard, 118, 161
Crazy to Act, **27**
Crosby, Bing, 154
Cubin, Bill, 174
Cushing, Peter, 116

Dahlberg, Mae, 17, 21, 23, 26, 112, 161
Dancing Masters, The, 146, **146**, 147, **147**, 163
Dandoe, Arthur, **13**, 16
Dann, Larry, 174
Danson, Ted, 136
Dardis, Tom, 127
Davidson, Max, 42, 162
Davies, Marion, 19
Davis, Mildred, 130
Day, Ron, 174
Delair, Suzy, 155
Delfont, Bernard, 152, 168
DeMille, Cecil B., 162
Dirty Work, 94, 175
Do Detectives Think?, 9, 43
Double Whoopee, 54, 59, **59**, 162
Down on the Farm, 157
Duck Soup, 9, 28, 77

Early to Bed, 50, **52**
Edwards, Blake, 136
Edwards, Ralph, 168
Egg, The, **23**
Electra Glide in Blue, 163
Ellis, Patricia, 199, 110
Ensminger, Robert, **32**
Enough to Do, 27
Errol, Leon, 162

Face the Music (TV), 165
Fairbanks, Douglas, 35, 152
Fall Guy, The, **18**
Feet First, 130
Fields, W.C., 39
Fighting Kentuckian, The, 153, 154
Films and Filming, 102, 133
Fine Mess, A, 136
Finishing Touch, The, 43, **46**, **47**
Finlayson, James, 27, **39**, 41, 42, **42**, 54, 56, **58**, 64, 68, **73**, 75, 77, 78, 81, 82, 93, 102, 105, 107, **107**, 109, 114, 117, **156**, 157, 159, 162
Fixer Uppers, The, 99
Flying Deuces, The, 112, **114**, **115**
Foolish Wives, 157
Fortune's Mask, 30, **32**, 84
Foy, Eddie, 159
Fra Diavolo, **92**, 93, 95, 102, 159
Fragson, Harry, 29
Freeman, Howard, 141
Freshman, The, **128**, 152
From Soup to Nuts, 43

Gable, Clark, 162
Gallagher, J.P., 12
Gamora, Charles, **88**
Gardiner, Reginald, 112
Garvin, Anita, 43, 68, 77, 159, **159**, 160

Gentle Cyclone, 19, **22**
Gentlemen Prefer Blondes (Loos), 127
General, The, 41, 124, 126, 127
Get 'Em Young, 27
Gilbert, Billy, 85, 109, 161, 162
Gilbert, John, 60
Girl Rush, 163
Glass Key, The, 163
Going Bye-Bye, 96, **96**
Gold Rush, The, 123
Gombell, Minna, 110
Go West, 126
Grable, Betty, 144
Grandma's Boy, 128
Grant, Cary, 115
Great Dictator, The, 123
Great Guns, 137, **138, 139**, 140, 163
Great Race, The, 136
Grey, Lita, 123
Grierson, John, 134
Griffith, D.W., 124, 161, 162
Guiles, Fred Lawrence, 11, 60, 101, 111
Guys and Dolls (stage), 144

Habeas Corpus, 52
Hadfield, Mark, 174
Hale, Alan, 105
Hall, Charlie, 41, 43, 85, 99, 118, **160**, 161
Hall, Henry, 165
Handy Man, **24**
Hardy, Myrtle, 26, 60, 112
Hardy, Oliver Sr, 17
Hardy, Mrs Oliver Sr, 17
Hardy, Lucille, 112, 152, 170, 171
Harlow, Jean, 54, 59, 60, 162
Harvey, Forrester, 116
Hatley, Marvin, 92, 107
Hats Off, 43, 84
Healy, Betty, 105
Hell's Angels, 162
Helpmates, 82, **84**, 174, 175
Henry, Charlotte, **97**
Herbert, Victor, 96
Hill, Hannah, 121
Hill, Jack, 161
Hog Wild, 71, **72**, 175
Holderness, Fay, 71
Hold That Ghost, 140
Hollywood Party, 162
Hoose-Gow, The, 65, **66**
Horne, James W., 56
Houdini, Harry, 124
Housman, Arthur, 97, 161
Hughes, Howard, 162
Hurley, Edgar, 16
Hurley, Wren, 16

In Cold Blood, 163
Intolerance, 124
Ireland, Ian, 174

Janney, William, 102
Jansen, Harry A., 140
Jazz Singer, The, 37, 43, 60
Jefferson, A. J., 11, 12, 13, 16
Jefferson, Gordon, 16

Jefferson, Margaret, 11
Jessell, George, 159
Jimmy the Fearless (stage), 12
Jitterbugs, 144, **145**
Jolson, Al, 37, 159
Jones, Buck, 19, **22**
Jones, Lucille (see Hardy, Lucille)

Kaye, Danny, 170
Karno, Fred, 12, 13, 16, 19, 29, 121
Karno, Fred Jr, **13**
Keaton, Buster, 22, 29, 35, 39, 118, 121, 123-7, **125**, 128, 130, 131, 132, 135, 136, 171
Keaton, Harry, 124
Keaton, Joe, 123, 124
Keaton, Louise, 124
Keaton, Myra, 124
Keith, Isabelle, 77
Kelly, Patsy, 161
Kelsey, Guy, **111**
Kennedy, Edgar, 20, **45**, 50, 52, 59, 60, 63, 64, **67**, 121, 141, 161, **161**
Kerr, Walter, 29, 32, 34, 128
Kid, The, 126
Kid Auto Races at Venice, 121
Kid Brother, The, 130
Kid Speed, 19
Kilgore, Al, 170
King, Dennis, 93, 159
King, Steve, 166
King, Walter Woolf, 108
Knight, Felix, 97
Knowles, R.G., 31

Ladd, Alan, 140, 163
Landwehr, Michael, 174
Lang, June, 102
Langdon, Harry, 9, 10, 111, **111**, 130, 154
Laughing Gravy, 77, **77, 79**
Laurel and Hardy Murder Case, The, 69, 71, **72, 73**
Laurel and Hardy Revue, The (stage), 137
Laurel Before Hardy (Owen-Pawson, Mouland), 11
Laurel, Lois (wife), 27, 60
Laurel, Lois (daughter), 27, **101**
Laurel, Ida, 152, **164**, 170, 171
Laurel, Illeana, 112
Laurel, Virginia Ruth, 101, 112
Laurel, Stan Jr, 27, 101
Lawrence, Rosina, 106, 107, **107**
Lauder, Alec, 157
Leave 'Em Laughing, 45, **44, 45**
Lederer, Otto, 49
Leland, David, 152
Leo, Ted, 16
Lewis, Jerry, 136
Liberty, 54, **55**, 162
Lights of New York, 60
Lind, Della, 108
Lipson, Mark, 68
Live Ghost, The, 97
Lloyd, Harold, 20, 29, 39, 118, 126, 128-30, **129**, 131, 152
Lloyd, Marie, 29

London, Jean 'Babe', 78
Long, Walter, **80**, 81, **84**, 97, 161
Loos, Anita, 127
Loredo, Linda, 68
Love 'Em and Weep, 41, 77, 159
Lubitsch, Ernst, 144, 159
Lucas, Wilfred, 116
Lucky Dog, **16**, 17, 19, 165
Lufkin, Sam, 54, 161
Lyn, Jacqui, **89**
Lynne, Sharon, 107

Mabel's Strange Predicament, 121
McCabe, John, 9, 12, 16, 26, 27, 51, 132, 134, 137, 149, 155, 165, 166, 170, 174
McCarey, Leo, 9, 10, 20, 22, 28, 34, 39, 43, 54, 56, 71
MacDonald, Edmund, 140
McFarland, Spanky, **99**
McGrath, Tom, 174
Mackaill, Dorothy, 157
McNally, Stephen, 141
Making a Living, 121
Mandel, Howie, 136
Marshall, Trudy, 146
Martin, Dean, 136
Mast, Gerald, 11, 32
Maté, Rudolph, 106
Meek, Donald, 141
Meins, Gus, **97**
Men o'War, 63, **64, 65**
Merivale, Philip, 152
Midnight Patrol, **93**
Milky Way, The, 130
Miller, Patsy Ruth, **32**
Minter, Mary Miles, 123
Mr Laurel and Mr Hardy (McCabe), 9, 166
Mr Laurel and Mr Hardy (stage), 174
Mitchum, Robert, 146, **147**, 163
Modern Times, 123
Moffat, Graham, 157
Monroe, Marilyn, 162
Monsieur Beaucaire, 22
Monsieur Don't Care, 22
Morecambe, Eric, 136, 165, 168
Morecambe and Wise, 32, 34, 92
Moreland, Mantan, 140
Morris, Chester, 78
Morse, Viola, 26, 60, 112
Moss, H.E., 12
Movie Crazy, 130
Mud and Sand, 19, **23**
Mumming Birds (stage), 12, 13
Music Box, The, 43, 71, 84, 85, **87**, 161, 174, 175

Navigator, The, 39, 124, 126
Nelson, Dick, 140
Night in an English Music-hall, A (stage), 13, 16
Night Owls, **67**, 69, 165
Normand, Mabel, 121, 123
Nothing But Trouble, 150, **150, 151**, 152
Nuts in May, 17

Oakland, Vivien, **89**
Of Mice and Men, 115
Oliver the Eighth, **95**
Olsen and Johnson, 162
One Good Turn, 82, **82**
One Million B.C., 115
One Million Years B.C., 115
One Week, 126
On the Wrong Trek, 162
Our Gang, 20, 23, 99, 163
Our Hospitality, 124
Our Relations, **102**, **105**, 106, 134
Our Wife, **78**
Owen-Pawson, Jenny, 11
Owst, Ken, 153

Pack Up Your Troubles, 85, **89**
Pardon Us, 78, **80**, 81, 85
Parker, Jean, 112
Parrott, Charles (see Chase, Charley)
Parrott, James (Paul), 51, 71
Parry, Harvey, 128
Paule, Nicky, 174
Payson, Blanche, 69
Pembroke, Gertrude, 26
Pembroke, Perce, 26
Perfect Clown, The, **21**
Perfect Day, 64, 71, 175
Pickford, Mary, 152
Pitts, ZaSu, 161, 162
Playhouse, The, 126
Playmates, 19
Pollard, Daphne, 99, 105
Pollard, Snub, 20, 162
Powell, Jane, 159
Price, Kate, **21**
Price, Lucille Hardy (see Hardy, Lucille)
Professor Beware, 130
Public Enemy, 162
Putting Pants on Philip, 9, 29, **36**, 37, 39, 50

Ralston, Vera, **153**, 154
Read, Bob, 16
Real Tinsel, The (Rosenberg, Silverman), 26
Reeves, Alf, 13
Reiner, Carl, 136
Rent Collector, The, **17**
Retford, Ella, 29
Rhodes, Georgette, 68
Riding High, 154
Rio Rita, 135
Rise and Fall of American Humor, The (Bier), 134
Ritz Brothers, The, 162
Roach, Hal E., 9, 10, 20, **20**, 21, 22, 23, 27, 28, 30, 34, 39, 41, 43, 56, 59, 60, 99, 101, 102, 108, 111, **112**, 115, 128, 130, 134, 135, 136, 137, 159, 161, 170
Roach, Hal Jr, 115, 168
Roberts, Florence, 96, **97**
Rock, Joe, 26, 27
Rogers, Virginia Ruth (see Laurel, Virginia Ruth)
Rogers, Will, 20

Rogue Song, The, 71, **72**
Royal Wedding, 159
Rupert of Hee-Haw, 22
Rupert of Hentzau, 22
Ryan, Sheila, 140

Safety Last, 128
Sailors, Beware!, 41, 162
St Clair, Malcolm, 144, 146, 147, 149
Saloshin, Madelyn, 19
Sandford, Tiny, 58, **58**, 71, 161
Saphead, The, 124
Saps at Sea, 117, **117**, 118
Sawmill, The, 19
Schenck, Joseph M., 124, 126, 127
Schenck, Nick, 126
Scott, Malcolm, 29
'Scram!', **89**, 136, 161, 175
Second Hundred Years, The, 41, **41**, 42, 65
Sellers, Peter, 136
Semon, Larry, 17, **18**, 19, **21**, 130
Sennett, Mack, 9, 16, 20, 21, 111, 121, 124, 128, 157, 159, 161
Shane, 163
Sheard, Philip, 136, 166
Shedden, John, 174
Sherlock Jr., 39, 124
Short, Mr and Mrs, 11
Should Married Men Go Home?, 50
Silent Clowns, The (Kerr), 32
Sins of Harold Diddlebock, The, 130
Sleeping Beauty (stage), 12
Slipping Wives, 39
Small Town Idol, 157
Smithy, 22
Snow White and the Seven Dwarfs, 162
Soilers, The, 22
Sons of the Desert, **95**, 162
Space, Arthur, 149
Spoilers, The, 22
Stan and Ollie (stage), 174
Steamboat Bill Jr., 124, 126, 127
Steinbeck, John, 115
Sterling, Ford, 121, 157
Stevens, George, 39, 43, 54, 56, 136
Sugar Daddies, **39**
Summerville, Slim, 121
Swiss Miss, 108, **109**

Talmadge, Constance, 126
Talmadge, Natalie, 124, 126, 127
Talmadge, Norma, 126, 152
Talmadge, Peg, 127
Taylor, Sam, 152
Taylor, William Desmond, 123
Tell Them Willie Boy Is Here, 163
That's My Wife, 56, **57**
Their First Mistake, **90**
Their Purple Moment, 50, **50**, **51**
Them Thar Hills, **96**, 97
Thicker Than Water, 99
This Gun For Hire, 163
Three Ages, 124
Three Stooges, The, 162
Tibbett, Lawrence, 71

Tit for Tat, **99**
To Be Or Not To Be, 159
Todd, Thelma, 63, 77, 93, 102, 159, 161, 162
Toler, Sidney, 105
Topper, 115
Tosi, Luigi, 155
Toto the Clown, 21
Towed in a Hole, 85
Tracy, Spencer, 162
Tree in a Test Tube, The, **142, 143**, 144
Turpin, Ben, 78, 118, 157
Twice Two, **91**
Two Tars, 51, **53**, 56, 71, 175
Tynan, Kenneth, 165, 166

Unaccustomed as We Are, 63, 111, 159
Under Two Flags, 22
Under Two Jags, 22, 26
Unkissed Man, The, 162

Valentino, Rudolph, 19, 161
Van Dyke, Dick, 136, 152, 170
Velez, Lupe, 162, 163
Von Stroheim, Erich, 159

Walker, H.M., 43, 56, 71
Waller, Kenneth H., 174
Warren, Earle, 33
Wayne, John, **153**, 154
Way Out West, 106, 107, **107, 108**, 134, 174
Wedding Party, The (radio), 111
We Faw Down, 54, 111
Weissmuller, Johnny, 162
Welburn, Thomas, 153
Welch, Raquel, 115
West, Billy, 19
Wheeler and Woolsey, 135, 136
Wheeler, Bert, 135, 136
When Knighthood Was in Flower, 19
When Knights Were Cold, 19, **25**
White, Jacqueline, 141
White, Pearl, 35
Whitelaw, Arthur, 174
Whyberd, Albert, 12
Why Girls Love Sailors, 174
Wills, Chill, 107
Wise, Ernie, 32, 34, 93, 132, 134, 136, 165, 168
With Love and Hisses, 41
Wizard of Oz, The, 19, **21**
Wood, Wee Georgie, 12
Woode, Margo, **150**
Woolsey, Robert, 135, 136
Wow-Wows, The (stage), 13
Wrong Again, 54, 56, **56**

Yes, Yes, Nanette, 27
Young, Roland, 115
You're Darn Tootin', 43, **48, 49**, 134, 175

Zenobia, 111, **111**, 130, 154
Ziegfeld, Florenz, 135